SIX

# A
# FOOTBALL COACH'S
# JOURNEY TO A
# NATIONAL RECORD
# MARC RASMUSSEN

SOUTH DAKOTA STATE HISTORICAL SOCIETY PRESS

Pierre

# SIX

This publication is funded, in part, by the Great Plains Education
Foundation, Inc., Aberdeen, S.Dak.

Library of Congress Cataloging-in-Publication Data
Rasmussen, Marc, 1959–
Six : a football coach's journey to a national record / by Marc
Rasmussen.
    p. cm.
Includes bibliographical references and index.
ISBN 978-0-9845041-4-5
1. Welsh, Bill, 1903–1980. 2. Football coaches—South Dakota—
Claremont—Biography. 3. Football—South Dakota—Claremont—
History. 4. Six-man football—South Dakota—Claremont—History.
5. Claremont (S.D.)—History—Sources. I. Title.
GV939.W367R37 2011
796.332′092—dc23
[B]                                        2011019166

The paper in this book meets the guidelines for permanence
and durability of the committee on Production Guidelines for
Book Longevity of the Council on Library Resources.
Printed in the United States of America
Text and cover design by Rich Hendel

Please visit our website at www.sdshspress.com

15  14  13  12  11   1  2  3  4  5

*To*

Coach Willis ("Bill") Welsh,

*the grandfather I never knew,*

*and to the amazing athletes*

*of Claremont, South Dakota,*

*too long relegated to anonymity*

# CONTENTS

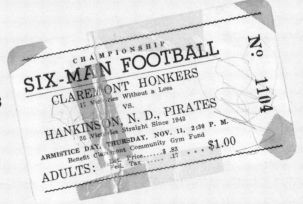

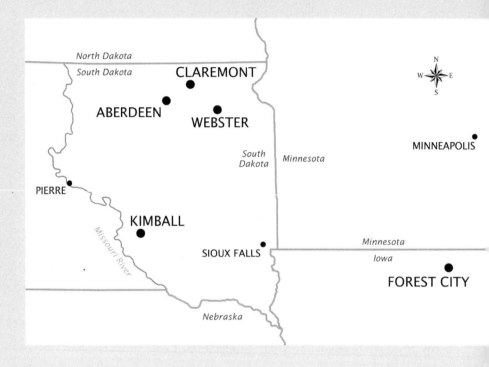

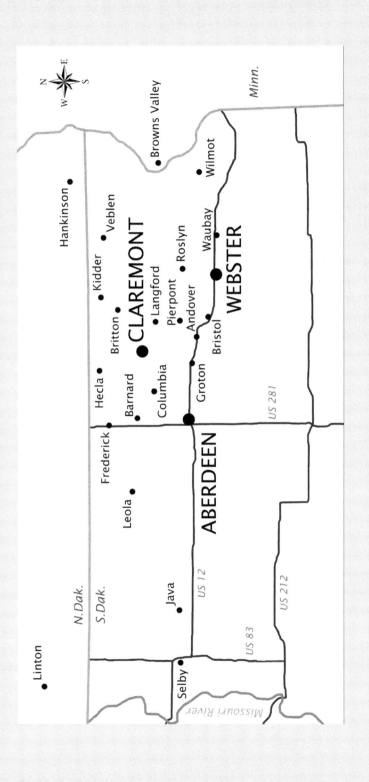

Examining the history and collecting the materials needed to write this book was an amazing experience for me. The project began simply enough as I started gathering background information to support the nomination of my father, Marvin Rasmussen, to the South Dakota Sports Hall of Fame. I had heard the stories of the high-school teams my father had competed on, but in his typically modest way, he never gave me all the details of just how special these groups of players were. Frankly, I was shocked by what these farm boys from northeastern South Dakota achieved.

I knew Claremont, South Dakota, as a small town where I went to visit my relatives in the summertime and for holidays. The town was but a shell of its former self, with a main street devoid of business activity except for a bank, restaurant, pool hall, and two grain elevators. There was also a meat locker, a gas station, two churches, and until I was eleven years old, a school. My family and I visited frequently and came to know the descendants of the athletes of Dad's generation. The names of those who had made Claremont special were well known to me, but what I did not understand was how important those names were to a generation of Dakotans who had observed their amazing performances on the football fields around the Upper Great Plains. As a boy, it was hard for me to imagine a town of such modest means fielding sports teams capable of achieving national records, but Claremont was an extraordinary place, and its residents accomplished extraordinary things.

One of the greatest rewards I received in writing this book was the discovery of a whole new family. My father's relationship with the key character in this story, Coach Willis ("Bill") Welsh, bordered on that between father and son. They had been close enough that Welsh's daughters always considered my father as their brother, and in my interactions with these incredible women, I became their nephew by association. My beloved "aunties" made the hard work of writing this book worthwhile. I therefore owe much to Jane Welsh Edwards, Judy Welsh Harmon, Patty Welsh Johnson, Billie Welsh Bartlett, and Jeannine Welsh Shea. In addition, Patty's son Mark Johnson was a great resource. A scrapbook prepared by Welsh's daughters detailing his life was foundational to the story, and their assistance in editing the material contributed greatly to the final product, as well. Their perspective was critical in telling, not just Welsh's story, but that of his son Jean, his wife Edna, and other important people in his life.

In the course of research, I was also honored to interview a number of players, cheerleaders, and fans of the great Claremont teams and to gain their support in presenting as accurate a tale as possible. I used much of their material in the Introduction to reflect a day in the life of the Claremont Honkers and capture the excitement of a big game. To aid me in the task, I was given access to such treasures as Mickey Vickers's scrapbook, prepared by his mother Ruby Vickers between the years

At a reunion in 2003, a group of players lined up one last time. *Marvin Rasmussen Collection*

1947 and 1949. Not only did she carefully cut articles from the newspapers, she also wrote her own impressions of the events and commentary about performance of the players. Harold ("Red") Sanderson provided additional information including football scores, articles, and background information from his scrapbooks from 1947 to 1950. Marvin Rasmussen's film of a group of former Honkers (Lyle Cutler, Warren Pearson, Kay Cutler, Donnie Gibbs, Gus Perkins, Marvin Rasmussen, Red Sanderson, and Bill James) who got together in 2003 to reminisce about the teams of yore. Their conversations provided a wealth of information about the practice habits of the team, how they learned to execute so effectively, the structure of their playbook, details of their pre-game warm-up, and Welsh's practice of telling stories of heroic performers to motivate his teams, although the specifics of these stories were left to me to extrapolate.

Delores Henihan, a member of the Claremont High School staff while Bill Welsh coached there, provided an excellent perspective of the coach's style and demeanor and the "flow" of the school day. Ramona Daly Hurin, one of the original Claremont cheerleaders, shared a substantial cache of data, old pho-

A number of Honkers from Welsh's teams gathered in 2003 to celebrate their achievements. *Marvin Rasmussen Collection*

tographs, and Claremont High School annuals. She also provided the details related to how the cheerleaders were taught to cheer and the impact of Welsh and his family on the cheerleading squad as they worked to educate the Claremont crowd on the nuances of the game of six-man football. Minute details of how games were staged came predominantly through conversations with Mickey Vickers, Jane Welsh Edwards, and Marvin Rasmussen.

I would be remiss if I failed to mention the stories of the Honkers teams as told by the morning coffee crowd at Swede's Bar in Langford, South Dakota. This group of area farmers and townsfolk provided the perspective of a town that was forever at the mercy of the Claremont teams. These good natured folks hosted me a number of times in discussions about the Honkers, and the price for their time was the opportunity to roll the dice to see who paid for the day's coffee. Somehow the rules changed frequently enough to leave me scratching my head and pulling out my wallet to peals of laughter from the assembled crowd.

Kamden Miller, the head basketball coach at Kimball High School, and the Kimball High School Administration helped me obtain photographs and data from Welsh's time there as coach. The photographs of these teams are used with their permission. Jim Block, principal/superintendent of Webster High School, was a key source of information, providing access to the athletic records given on an annual basis to the South Dakota State High School Athletic Association.

Monte Nipp, superintendent/principal of the Langford Public Schools, was kind enough to provide access to all team photographs, trophies, records, and information remaining from the Claremont School. This material had been transferred to the Langford School when Claremont closed its doors in 1970. The students from Claremont became Langford Lions the following year. A key pamphlet produced by the Claremont

Booster Club in 1951, detailed all the Claremont victories up to the point of the team setting the national record for consecutive wins. Beyond the team records and scores, it provided detail on the number of six-man teams competing in South Dakota at the time of the record.

Specific individuals who have not been previously mentioned include Brett Gibbs, John Papendick of the *Aberdeen American News*, Arlan Warwick, Gary Rasmussen, Bernie Hunhoff of *South Dakota Magazine*, Verl Cutler, Mel Klein, Coach Dale Brown of Louisiana State University (retired), Nick Leigh, Bob King, Al Neuharth, Ron Hoffman of the South Dakota Sports Hall of Fame, George Kiner from Coaches Against Cancer, the South Dakota State Library, my beloved wife Gail, and amazing daughter Nicole Remish. Also I give thanks to G. C. Groves, my grandfather, who helped me understand the rich history of South Dakota sports, and to my father, Marvin Rasmussen, one of those athletes to whom this book is dedicated.

Without the contributions of these individuals and many others, this book could not have come to life.

The wind blew cold through the broken cornstalks near the city limits, creating a dry rustling sound all too familiar to the residents of Claremont. This music of late fall was clear evidence that winter lurked right around the corner. It had been a good year for the farmers, and the harvest nestled safely in the bins, leaving the stubble to capture winter moisture for the benefit of next year's crop. The strong wind dislodged tumbleweeds from the fence lines and sent them on a frantic journey across the open fields to find a new resting place. High overhead, thousands of migrating ducks and geese swept south in tight "V" formations. Instinct told them that they had overstayed their welcome in this harsh land and that they should resume their long journey. Their distant calls taunted the wingless ones below, who were unable to escape the oncoming storm.

Clouds rolled in from the south and west, but as the temperature dropped, the wind direction changed. Frosty air descended from Canada on a collision course with moist air from the Gulf of Mexico creating perfect conditions for snow. South Dakota represented the eternal battlefield between these two weather masses, and the effect was often spectacular and sometimes deadly. The prospect of winter weather on 11 November 1948 did not make headlines in this part of the world, but it was not a popular development for fans of football on this important day.

The students walking to school felt the frigid breeze, and those without hats or scarves pulled their collars up around their ears as a defense against the chill. The school bell rang to signal the start of classes, and excitement filled the hallways as the forty students of Claremont High School shuffled into their homerooms. Extra color was evident throughout the school as most of the teenagers wore Claremont colors to express their support for their beloved Honkers football squad, and one inspired soul arrived early to scrawl "GO HONKERS" in big flowing letters on all the chalkboards.

The teachers met in the lounge just prior to the first class and moaned about how little the students would accomplish this day. One teacher suggested that a pop quiz would get their minds into learning, but her peers helped her understand her error. They knew that, even with the best of intentions, the children could not focus on anything but the upcoming game with mighty Hankinson, a team of athletes touted by the North Dakota press as the finest in both Dakotas.

Coach Willis ("Bill") Welsh, wearing his ever-present suit and tie, arrived early to make sure all the preparations for the upcoming game were complete. He walked through the halls amidst hails of "Good luck this afternoon, Coach" and "Knock 'em dead, Coach." His upright posture and composed demeanor gave a sense of calm to those who watched him pass. Welsh had a reassuring presence, and rarely did he need to raise his voice to the students to achieve complete attention. Willis Welsh, or Bill, as most people knew him, was intent on the completion of his tasks this morning, and his pace quickened as he saw the clock on the wall. He had a history class to teach, and the coach was never late.

Welsh had much to do in his roles of teacher and coach, and with a limited staff, he often deputized the townsfolk to help stage athletic events. He coordinated many volunteers anytime a big event took place, and today was a big event indeed. The coach discovered years before the importance of involving the community in building a successful sports program, and their participation in the staging of the game not only helped the school, but also inspired the students. He took the short walk to the football field located a block from the school and saw his miniature army of helpers already at work. Everyone was eager for the upcoming contest because this game really meant something; the teams were playing for what Welsh had dubbed the "Mythical Three-State Football Championship."

The talents of Bill Welsh were many, but one of his finest was an ability to promote athletic events. He always looked for interesting angles to boost attendance and had proven his ability to generate support from the fans. The revenue stream from ticket sales and donations from local boosters had already made possible a brand-new gym, just completed, adjacent to the Claremont High School. The 1948 Armistice Day game would be part of a larger celebration that included the formal opening of the new facility. The Claremont Gym Association had been formed at Welsh's urging during the summer of 1947, and as an example of the community's support, within a single week, the association acquired funding to construct the facility from ninety-seven farmers and local residents, some giving as much as five hundred dollars. Not satisfied with just funding the gym's construction, Welsh planned to cover ongoing expenses by operating a roller rink on the gym floor two nights a week; he even coordinated skating lessons for those interested. He planned to get various waltz records and work with his daughter Jane to create dance steps to the music. Later, because of this effort, the girls of Claremont created the first dance/skating team in the area, and they would perform to "Cruising Down the River" by Russ Morgan for the halftime entertainment at home basketball games.

The coach paused for a moment as he gazed at the gym and reflected on what this project meant to the community. Like an old-fashioned barn-raising, the construction of the facility brought together the local population. The gym featured a forty-two by seventy-six foot playing surface and was equipped with two lavatories, two locker rooms, a stage, and an annex in which a fully functional kitchen provided concessions during basketball games. Nearly twice the size of the old floor in the Legion Hall, the court seemed huge to the players, who were used to the old surface where the top of both keys actually touched the center circle on the floor.

Welsh shook his head when he recalled their first attempt to prepare the new floor for basketball. The builders chose to glue Masonite tiles directly to the concrete underlying the floor. It made sense on paper, but the amateur engineers of Claremont were unable to get the tiles to remain secured to the concrete. Lest the tiles come off in the midst of an important game, the builders came up with Plan B. The solution was to create a faux playing surface over the concrete with a framework of two-by-fours covered with plywood, to which they glued and nailed the tiles. It satisfied all who competed in the gym. The seating had also been dramatically improved. In the Legion Hall, less than seventy-five spectators could view a game, but in the new gym, as many as twelve hundred fans could cram in to see the Honkers play. The 1948 Armistice Day football game was part of a two-day long carnival to celebrate the gym's official opening. After the Honkers had taken on Hankinson, the townspeople would convene in the gym for a celebratory dinner, at which Mylo Jackson, head coach of the Aberdeen Central Golden Eagles, would be the featured speaker.

In assessing the potential crowd for the game versus Hankinson, Welsh knew attendance would not be a problem. Automobiles and pickup trucks already surrounded the playing field, parked in a rectangle just a few feet outside the grid lines. Some industrious entrepreneurs even backed a one-ton flatbed truck up to the field to provide a platform for those willing to pay an extra quarter for an improved vantage point. The uninitiated might imagine a drive-in movie was on the schedule, or perhaps a parking lot had spontaneously appeared, for the sight of so many empty cars neatly surrounding a bare field seemed odd. Eager fans seeking a good seat for the upcoming game had parked their cars the previous day or earlier that morning. Prior to floodlights and dedicated bleachers being commonplace in high-school stadiums, cars served multiple functions. They offered shelter from the cold, a place to sit when bleacher seats were limited, and a source of light as the days grew shorter; the headlights making it possible to finish late-running contests. The cars also created some interesting endings to plays that took the athletes out of bounds. Now and then, players slid under a big old Chevy rather than plow into one of the huge fenders, bumpers, or running boards, and occasionally, the marks of cleats were seen on a car's hood as a youngster took the high road over the paint job to dissipate his momentum.

Welsh proceeded across the field to speak with the man busily outlining the dimensions of the playing field with white chalk lines. The coach reminded him to bring some black coal dust that afternoon so that the lines would not disappear under a white blanket of snow. The volunteers carried a nervous energy about them. Over the past two seasons, the community had become as much a part of the team as the players, and each person helping to prepare for the game had sympathetic butterflies in the stomach for their young athletes. These extended team members each played a role in making the event special, whether taking tickets, running the concession stand,

Cars lined the field to provide seating and light, if needed. *Marvin Rasmussen Collection*

or directing traffic. Each volunteer earned his own nickname, provided by Welsh, to match his job. For instance, he called the ticket taker, "Scalper," and the man who marked the field, "Lineman."

This game would be Welsh's second Armistice Day contest as head of the Claremont Honkers athletic programs. In the first, the year before, the Honkers defeated a tough team from Montrose (twenty-five miles west of Sioux Falls) by a score of 40 to 24. Montrose had come to Claremont with a ten-game winning streak and with limited respect for the upstart team from northeastern South Dakota that lacked even a full season of six-man football in its short history. Featuring Bill Griffith, an unstoppable 220-pound fullback, Montrose had found it hard to take seriously a group of athletes wearing sweatshirts with numbers painted on them rather than the proper jerseys enjoyed by wealthier school districts.

The handbills, written by Welsh, advertised the game as a championship contest: "Montrose boasts one of the finest teams in South Dakota being undefeated and untied at present in one of South Dakota's toughest conferences. Claremont has a great record, winning seven straight without defeat and winner of undisputed championship of the North Central Conference. See these two undefeated 6-man teams battle for the Mythical 6-Man Championship (of South Dakota)." Even though Claremont had won all of its games preceding this contest, the Montrose team was supremely confident, and Claremont's homemade jerseys helped lull them into a state of complacency. When the final gun sounded, however, performance had won out over dress as the Montrose team fell hard to this group of ragamuffins, giving the Honkers the first of many unofficial state championships.

Despite their convincing victory and their undefeated season, there was some controversy to the Honkers' claim over the championship; the six-man team from Selby had also gone undefeated during the 1947 season. Selby's team and fans crowed about being a co-champion because of their record, and their claims made the newspapers. Welsh, being the consummate promoter, recognized the opportunity in this situation and called Herb Bjella, the Selby coach, and invited the Lions to play the Honkers early in the 1948 season. The result removed all doubt about the previous year's championship, with Claremont defeating Selby by a score of 68 to 14. It was Selby's first loss in two years, and the game was one of many stiff challenges that Welsh accepted during the course of what would become a seven-year, sixty-one game, national-record-setting winning streak.

Due to the Honkers' success in their first season, Claremont's residents purchased new uniforms, assuring that the Honkers not only played like winners but looked the part as well. In fact, the success of the Honker program created some logistical problems for Welsh. After a game, Welsh received the proceeds from ticket and concession sales to deposit in the bank the next day or the following Monday if a game fell on a weekend. Given the large gate receipts the Honkers were earning by the end of their second season, Welsh became concerned about attracting a thief looking for an easy score and came up with a novel solution to counter the risk. He had four individuals count the money after the game back at the school. Each of the counters would prepare a moneybag, but only one of the bags would actually contain the money. The four people would then take the bags to the coach's house using different routes. Once the coach had the proceeds, he would wrap them in butcher paper, mark the package as hamburger, and put it into the freezer. After a particularly big game, he was not even comfortable with that routine and decided to stuff it into a turkey thawing in the refrigerator to throw off even the most cunning thief. Ultimately, the owner of the local bank agreed to pick up the funds after games, which proved a huge relief to the coach and his family.

Today's game, on 11 November 1948, was also destined to attain big proceeds. The opposition from Hankinson had dominated the six-man game in North Dakota for the past six years, and the team had a large fan following. Coached by Arch Earnest, Hankinson had recorded an amazing forty-one wins, two losses, and two ties, and had won thirty-seven of the past thirty-eight games. The only loss came at the hands of the team from West Fargo, North Dakota, by a score of 12 to 8. Coach Welsh indicated, in one of his handbills advertising the game, that this six-man team had the best record in the country over that period. The Claremont faithful were all aware of the challenge facing their team. The Honkers carried their own streak into the game, however, having won each of its first seventeen games since it started playing six-man football in the fall of 1947. Earlier in the 1948 season, Claremont had also traveled to Browns Valley, Minnesota, where the Honkers had decisively defeated, by a score of 65 to 41, a team considered by many to be the best six-man team in Minnesota. Browns Valley, from the Little Six Conference, had brought an undefeated record into that game, having scored an average of fifty-five points per contest. They used power and size, rather than speed, to grind out wins. The two 190-pound Reed brothers carried the success of the team on their backs and accounted for most of Browns Valley's scoring. The game was as physical as any the Honkers had played to that date, and the victorious Claremont players nursed some real bruises on the long trip home that night.

By defeating Browns Valley, Welsh claimed his first unofficial South Dakota-Minnesota championship, and he now used this achievement to hype the contest against Hankinson. He understood that the buildup would produce an exciting and well-attended event. Welsh employed a small ritual when he won a big away game. He went to the school when the team returned to town and fired his shotgun into the air to signal to townsfolk that the mighty Honkers had returned victorious. After the Browns Valley win, signaled by two shots from an old double-barrel twelve-gauge shotgun, excited residents of Claremont, looking to hear the details, quickly joined him at the school.

In his unassuming way, he gave credit to everyone but himself, adding to the local enthusiasm for his team. While Welsh was not one to toot his own horn, his capable guidance had been just what this group of athletes needed to put them on the map. The win over Browns Valley, followed quickly by one over the undefeated squad from Faith (which the local press billed as the best team in western South Dakota, and who had traveled two hundred fifty miles for the game), set the stage for the 1948 season-ending game with Hankinson for bragging rights in the upper Midwest region.

As the reputation of the Honkers spread, more and more spectators from outside Claremont had started to come to the games. Attendance had grown by the week. Such was the Honkers' draw that the much larger Groton High School had invited the Honkers to play Faith in front of Groton's homecoming crowd. Groton competed in the eleven-man variety of the sport against much larger schools, but the organizers of the Tigers' annual Jungle Day celebrations understood what a goldmine the Honkers represented in terms of attendance. It was a brilliant strategy. The Honkers faithful, along with the Groton spectators and visitors, produced a large crowd in spite of the poor weather that day.

The contest against Hankinson at the end of the Honkers' second season represented an opportunity for Claremont to cement its program as the premier six-man team in the three-state region. It would prove beyond a doubt that the Claremont Honkers were worthy of their number-one ranking in South Dakota. This season had already seen an offensive explosion unlike any enjoyed by a six-man football team in the game's short history, including a seventy-seven-point performance against the Faith Longhorns, and six other scores of sixty-plus. Faith had held its opposition scoreless in the seven games preceding the 1948 contest with Claremont, but the scoreless streak ended just twenty-one seconds into the game. A handoff to Claremont's Donnie Gibbs resulted in a fifty-yard touchdown run, the first of six he scored that day. If the Honkers scored against Hankinson in a similar manner, they had a chance to set a national six-man single-season scoring record, a fact no one on the team was aware of at the time. Had they been aware, Welsh may have changed his substitution practices in earlier games to assure his team a place in football history before the final contest of the season. As in most Honkers' games, the first team only played part of the contest, with the seconds getting significant playing time, making Gibbs's scoring rate that day even more impressive.

As dawn broke on the morning of the Hankinson-Claremont game, the locals met for coffee in Claremont's tiny business district, which many did on a daily basis, providing folks with a chance to socialize with neighbors separated by miles of tilled fields. Conversations buzzed with the words Honkers and football. The laughter and energy from the assembled group spilled out into the street and carried to pedestrians making their way downtown. It enticed more than the normal number of people to join the party. The fans loved their Honkers; for the small price of admission, they received great entertainment.

Back at the school that day, true to the teachers' predictions, limited learning occurred. Lunch, loud and raucous, got out of hand, and Welsh reminded the students to act like ladies and gentlemen. The scheduled time for kickoff was 2:30 P.M. and excitement reached a crescendo as the final bell approached. At 1:00 P.M., fans began to congregate at the field, and the sound of cars starting and idling cut through the cold wind. In the days before emissions restrictions, the aroma of over-ripe exhaust blew across the field, making a few eyes water downwind. The booster club arrived early to brew coffee and heat apple cider and cocoa to keep the fans warm. A few of the old-timers stuffed flasks into their bib overalls to season their coffee with their favorite flavors. A little Old Grand-Dad bourbon in a hot cup of Maxwell House helped keep the cold at bay and complemented the unfiltered, hand-rolled cigarettes seemingly affixed to their bottom lips.

The bus from Hankinson arrived at 1:00 P.M., and the Honker fans showed a little concern when the North Dakota champions exited the bus and strutted into the visitor's locker room in the new Claremont gym. Their swagger had an intimidating effect on those who watched intently from the windows of the high school. Fans from Hankinson had followed the bus on its eighty-mile journey with bright royal-blue-and-white banners proudly flying in the wind. The Pirates' fans expected to witness nothing short of a coronation of their team as the champions of the region, and they happily shared their enthusiasm with those in earshot.

More than fourteen hundred people lived in Hankinson in the 1940s, and at least half of them made the trip to Claremont. The roughly two-hundred fifty residents of Claremont would certainly attend the game, and a good-sized cadre of fans from the surrounding area would join them at the spectacle. An entourage from Dickinson, North Dakota, had also crossed the border, and they added energy to the crowd as well. An *Aberdeen American News* reporter attending the crowd estimated that the

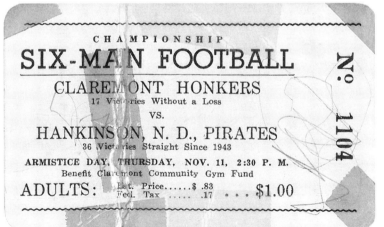

Welsh's volunteers printed formal tickets for each game. This example is for the showdown with Hankinson in 1948. *Mickey Vickers Collection*

crowd numbered close to two thousand spectators. The ticket takers were amazed as proceeds from sales swelled to over one thousand dollars, an outstanding total for a small-town athletic event. A half-hour before kickoff, a bus from nearby Oakes, North Dakota, arrived carrying the pre-game entertainment. It was the last ingredient in this well-planned event, and Welsh's army of volunteers could breathe easy and enjoy the game about to unfold.

The Honkers team assembled in the gym just after 1:00 P.M. Welsh appreciated the field of psychology and realized how excitement could affect young minds before a big event. He had learned many years before how to focus his players' attention on the task ahead and how to get their blood boiling in anticipation of the game. Welsh, a wonderful storyteller, drew the athletes' young heads out of the present and transported them to a place where David defeated Goliath on a routine basis. When he finished his stories, his players would be coursing with adrenaline and prepared to defeat all comers. Welsh used his vocal inflections as an instrument, and he chose his words carefully to gain the most emotional impact. His strong baritone voice came across clear and direct, and he spoke without hesitation, sounding more like a Shakespearian actor than a football coach. His athletes listened intently, noiseless, absorbing each word and living the images Welsh brought to life with his stories.

In the locker rooms of the new gym that day, the experienced coach told one of his favorite stories, which involved a young man raised on an Indian reservation in Oklahoma in the late 1800s and early 1900s. The young man was called Bright Path in his native language. His parents sent him and his brother to an Indian boarding school when both were young. The siblings were extremely close and did everything together. Not long after his ninth birthday, Bright Path's brother took ill and died suddenly of pneumonia, devastating the young survivor who found himself struggling to find any joy in his life. He begged to come home, but his parents would not allow it. Life became more unbearable when his mother died two years later while giving birth to another child. The young man ran away from school and wandered aimlessly, finally returning home to his father.

Encouraged to go back to school, Bright Path chose to attend the Carlisle Indian School in Carlisle, Pennsylvania, where he met a coach named Glenn ("Pop") Warner, who would ultimately be inducted into the College Football Hall of Fame for his accomplishments. In Bright Path's first year at Carlisle, the young man's father died of gangrene, leaving him an orphan. He was truly a lost soul, but just when it seemed darkest for him, he found his Indian name to be his guide. The young man discovered that his "bright path" was athletics and that he had a real talent for sports. One day, as he walked past some athletes preparing for a track meet, he watched them train for the high jump and asked if he could give it a try. Amidst snickers from those practicing, he lined up for his first jump. Wearing his street clothes and with no prior experience, he cleared the bar, beating the best of the group assembled. The spectators grew quiet, having gotten their first glimpse of an athlete who was to become a legend.

The Honkers' coach then related to his team that Bright Path's English name was Jim Thorpe, and that this legendary young man, who had faced the hardest challenges life could throw at him, found sports to be his salvation. Thorpe also played football, and took his team to a national collegiate championship, and during the course of his career, he earned two All-American Awards. Following such success, Thorpe tried out for the 1912 Olympic team, and in a stunning performance, won two gold medals and placed in two other events. After the Olympics, he became a professional baseball, football, and basketball player. From poor and painful beginnings, this young American Indian boy persevered to become the toast of the athletic world, a path that any one of the Honkers in that room had the potential to follow, Welsh assured them.

Welsh's young players took in every word, and by the time he finished his mini-biography of Jim Thorpe, the players hungered for their own chance at immortality. A mere game stood between them and the ability to accomplish something they had not dreamed of when they first touched a football two short years earlier. The twenty players, representing every male student in the high school, quickly dressed in their dark blue jerseys with red shoulders, white pants, and nice new helmets. Once dressed, they gathered for the pre-game chalk talk where Welsh went over the Xs and Os one more time. The huddle had grown by this time to include a group of excited but well-behaved grade- and middle-school boys, whom the coach allowed to listen in as long as they remained quiet. This junior assemblage of future stars is a fairly common sight at modern high-school athletic events, but Welsh had added the practice at a time when few other schools allowed such an indulgence, reasoning that in a tiny town he must reach deep into the student population to develop future players and what better way than by giving them exposure before they even began to compete. Welsh had actually decided to implement this practice when he took the position at Claremont. As a way of accepting and recovering from the death of his five-year-old son Jean, who had been hit by a car and died in 1943, Welsh sought comfort in helping to mold young minds.

The chalk talk ended, Welsh completed the preparations, and the team gathered for its grand entrance. Each player had his own way of getting ready, but Mickey Vickers used the most unusual method. Before every game, he took a moment to throw up any lunch that he had enjoyed that day, and today was no exception. Vickers returned from the bathroom wiping his mouth and joking about how this event might keep the Hankinson blockers from getting too close to him. Then the Honkers, led by their three best players, Donnie Gibbs, Neil Cain, and Vickers, sprinted the one block to the site of the contest and, making a quick lap around the field, stopped in front of the crowd to fire them up. The crowd clapped and cheered as the team began their warm-ups, with the captains leading the team through a series of calisthenics. For the seniors, it was the last football game of their high-school careers, in which none had experienced a loss. Warming up on that bitter cold day, the boys determined to end their careers with that status intact.

The Claremont crowd chattered excitedly, discussing strategy and basking in the fanfare. The hometown fans had come a long way since witnessing the first six-man football game of their lives just the previous season. Claremont residents understood baseball; the town's team had won the 1938 State Amateur Baseball championship. Early in the 1930s, the high school had also fielded a short-lived eleven-man football team, but during the first season of six-man football in 1947, the game had seemed so foreign to the players and the crowd that Welsh's father, his wife, and even his young daughter had to walk up and down the sidelines during the game, explaining the rules and answering questions.

The fans watched as the Honkers completed their exercises and the starting offensive team lined up against the seconds and began running through plays. Quarterback Neil Cain had started all the school's six-man football games. Donnie Gibbs lined up at fullback, with Mickey Vickers at halfback. Between them, the two young men had accounted for a large percentage of the record-setting number of touchdowns the Honkers had piled up during the past two years. At center stood big Willie Hollister, a mountain of a young man who opened holes in the defense and moved the pile forward. Bob Stanley and Lyle Cutler played the two ends. This core group of players had been life-long friends.

Gibbs, tall and handsome, had an infectious smile but was generally a quiet star, who self-deprecatingly kept his sporting accomplishments quiet, particularly when around strangers. Mickey Vickers was another exceptional athlete who excelled in football and baseball, probably acquiring some of his baseball-playing father's athletic genes. His father was one of three Vickers who propelled Claremont's amateur baseball team to the South Dakota championship in 1938 over a vaunted Aberdeen squad. Smaller than the others, but extremely quick, Mickey Vickers was more outgoing than his best friend Gibbs and was clearly the leader of the team. Vickers's good looks contributed to his having a steady girlfriend, Ramona Daly, throughout his high-school years. Neil Cain shared more character traits with Vickers than with Gibbs, and his classmates held him in high regard. On the field, Cain moved the offense as a general moves his troops, directing the play from his quarterback position. Vickers was the secondary scoring option and an accomplice to the well-crafted plays spun out by Welsh's offensive scheme, while Gibbs carried the scoring burden on his capable shoulders. Many years later, Vickers described his role on the team as being there to block for Gibbs, nothing more; even so, he enjoyed plenty of glory and responsibility for the wins. Willie Hollister, at center, provided the muscle in the middle, and his ability to block so effectively made possible many of the team's accomplishments.

Six-man football was a wide-open game designed for multiple scoring options, but with the strength of Claremont's running game, passing was just a minor part of the offense. Despite the run-first tendencies of Welsh's schemes, the Honkers scored heavily; even the two ends played scoring roles through the myriad end-around and reverse plays in the coach's playbook. Hollister even joined in the scoring occasionally. In six-man football, the center could score just like everyone else, and he sometimes took a short pass from the quarterback or the pitch back from one of the ends in a flea-flicker play.

One play Welsh designed for Hollister always seemed to produce good yardage. In the modern six-man game, the center snaps the ball to the quarterback with both facing forward, but all through Welsh's tenure at Claremont, the rules allowed for teams to snap the ball with the two players standing backside to backside. Using the back-to-back technique helped mask the intentions of the offensive players and provided a better platform for trickery. In the play designed for Hollister, Gibbs and Vickers crowded right in around Cain. When Hollister snapped the ball to Cain, the quarterback immediately placed the ball on the ground, and the three backs all ran in different directions, taking the attention of the defensive players with them. In the meantime, Hollister took a step back, picked up the ball, and started running downfield untouched by the defense. He rarely made it more than twenty yards before being tackled, but it nearly always produced a first down for the team and even an occasional touchdown.

On this cold Armistice Day, the crowd overflowed the seats and hung from any vantage point available, including a lucky few who found seats on top of the concession stand near the forty-yard line. As the temperature continued to drop, the fans huddled close in the stands or sat sheltered behind the big windows of the cars and trucks parked around the field. The youngsters stayed low at the front of the crowd, careful not to block the view of the grownups. Most sat cross-legged near the side-

This still from a 16mm film of the 1950 match-up against Hecla clearly shows the back-to-back snap technique. *Marvin Rasmussen Collection*

lines, taking in the spectacle and dreaming of the time when it would be their turn on the playing field. At halftime, they would erupt from their places, grab the loose footballs, and, as the teams huddled in the end zones, play catch in the hopes that the massive crowd was watching them.

The cheerleaders, dressed in coats, earmuffs, scarves, and mittens, began to warm up for the game, their muffled clapping swallowed in the midst of the crowd's excitement. The girls did not enjoy this cold weather, but they relied on their enthusiasm and routines to keep warm. The cheering squad had come a long way since the previous year when they had relied on Welsh's signals for when to cheer. None of the girls had seen a game of football before the 1947 season, and without the coach's guidance, they had not known when and for what to applaud. Understanding that he had to help stage the whole spectacle, Welsh would turn around when a big play occurred and signal the girls to execute a particular cheer that matched the situation.

The homemade goal posts stood sentinel in the end zones, each with a cross bar made of painted two-by-fours that sagged a bit in the middle. None of the spectators minded because they had come to see touchdowns, not field goals, and, in fact, the Honkers rarely chose a drop kick (the technique used in six-man) for the extra point; they excelled in running the ball in for the point after touchdown. The cheerleaders wrapped the goal posts in colored crepe paper, adding to an otherwise bland field made brown by the season. Before the game, the Drum and Bugle Corps from Oakes, North Dakota, performed with all the pomp and circumstance of a college game. They ended their performance with the national anthem, and the referee called the captains to the center of the field for the coin toss.

The umpire tossed the coin high into the air, where it caught the wind and landed behind the captains. The crowd clapped in approval when he signaled that Claremont had won the toss and elected to receive the ball. The Hankinson Pirates chose to have the wind at their back, thinking it would be a factor before the game ended. The teams took their places on the field, and the Pirates prepared for the kickoff. Coming in with such an excellent record of their own, the Hankinson players stood confidently as the referee prepared to blow his whistle, the prospect of defeat not entering their minds. The snow, which had held off to that point, began to fall. The Pirates' kicking team lined up, and because of the stiff breeze, one of the Hankinson players held the ball for the kicker. The referee's whistle signaled the start of play, and the wind carried the kickoff into Honkers' territory. On the first play from scrimmage, Gibbs took a pitch from Cain and immediately demonstrated what a six foot two inch athlete, weighing 190 pounds, who ran one of the fastest one-hundred-yard dashes in the state, could do. Heading right down the center of the field, Gibbs raced fifty yards for a touchdown, bypassing almost every Hankinson player with little difficulty along the way. Not used to such an imposing figure, the defenders could not get an angle on him to make the tackle. As Gibbs crossed the goal line, he turned to see the look of confusion on the faces of the defenders, and he smiled as if enjoying a private joke, knowing the visitors from North Dakota were in for a long afternoon.

The large contingent of fans from Hankinson watched in disbelief as the Honkers repeatedly fooled their defense with perfect execution and team speed. The North Dakotans were far too used to seeing their boys dominate anyone they opposed. Claremont's speed also wreaked havoc on the powerful Hankinson offense as the Honkers stuffed their runs and hounded their receivers, keeping the Pirates out of the end zone the entire game. The Pirates had one genuine scoring opportunity in the whole game, but fumbled the ball on the Honkers' one-yard line. By halftime, Claremont led 34 to 0. Gibbs had scored five touchdowns, and the Hankinson players who did find themselves in position to tackle him found out one of the reasons for his success. Gibbs preferred to deal out a bigger blow to his tackler than he received. Where lesser players may have gone down or run out of bounds, Gibbs instead angled towards the tackler and initiated contact. Given his size and speed, some defenders tended to hang back rather than try to wrap him up, resulting in even more touchdowns. As time ticked off the clock, it appeared that the only thing that could stop the Honkers was halftime. However, an unexpected whistle paused the game just before halftime, alerting the teams to the fact that Lineman needed to reline the field with coal dust, as the snow had made it impossible to see white chalk on the ground.

For the second half, Welsh sent out his "B" team. The damage had been done in the first two quarters, and the second half resulted in only one additional touchdown. When the final gun sounded, the dispirited Hankinson Pirates, tired of watching the back of the Honkers' helmets as they crossed the goal line ahead of them, had succumbed 40 to 0. The school colors of the Hankinson athletes seemed to have faded; their vivid blue and white appeared more black and blue, both figuratively and literally, as the muddy field left its mark, clinging hard to the Hankinson uniforms.

As soon as the game ended, Welsh trotted across the field to thank each Hankinson player individually for their effort, and he warmly embraced the hand of the Hankinson coach, telling him how much he appreciated their participation. Welsh always kept the game in perspective in order to model the best in sportsmanship for his players. Throughout his coaching career, he was the finest host and the most gracious winner an opposing coach could ask for, and he exhibited the same traits when he faced a rare loss. He taught his players that doing the right thing won out no matter what the final score read. As the Hankinson players boarded the bus for their return to North Dakota, the Claremont fans matched their coach's ideals and gave the visitors an ovation. Turning from the departing bus, Claremont fans walked to the school, where the Armistice

Day festivities and homecoming carnival got under way, with Merve's Swingsters, a local dance band, playing late into the evening.

With this victory, the Honkers earned the unofficial status of best six-man team in the Dakotas and Minnesota, and they did not relinquish these bragging rights until the end of 1953. With these forty points added to their totals from previous games, the 1948 Honkers set a national record by scoring 608 points over a ten-game season. A team from New York beat their record in 1950, but the Honkers' feat remains one of the greatest single-season scoring performances in the history of the sport.

The 1948 victory over Hankinson accounted for just one day in the history of a team that carried the national banner for the sport of six-man football for a seven-year period from 1947 to 1953. Claremont High School, with a student population that never exceeded forty, dominated the South Dakota sports scene and established a national record by winning sixty-one consecutive six-man football games. Their first win had come against the nearby Hecla Rockets in the fall of 1947, and their first loss would come nearly seven years later to the same Hecla squad. Even after the loss, the Honkers won an additional game that year, all the games the following year, and even the 1955 version of the team went undefeated. Their record over an eight-year period was seventy-eight wins and one loss for a winning percentage of 98.7 percent. Claremont's football team came from nowhere to dominate the sports pages on a local, state, and regional basis. The talented group of young men who made up the early teams contributed to the team's quick ascension, but they would not have achieved their success were it not for the addition of a certain coach.

The story of the Claremont Honkers six-man football team has almost been lost. The high school closed in 1970, a victim of the demise of small farms and resulting population outflow to more urban areas that has afflicted much of South Dakota.

All that remains of the school is a small brick archway erected as a monument to its past triumphs, with the name of each of the 451 students who attended Claremont High displayed on a plaque inlaid on the side. Standing sentinel atop the monument are the original school bell and a metal sculpture of a Canadian Honker situated on a steel I-beam with the words "Public School" cut out of it. In a vault at the bottom is a time capsule with instructions that it not be opened until 2070, the

Today, all that remains of Claremont High School is this small monument. *Marc Rasmussen Collection*

hundredth anniversary of the school's closure. Where the gym once stood only the concrete that lay under the playing surface remains. Two badly bent basketball goals with ripped nets stand forlornly. Leading to the archway is the same cracked sidewalk that bore the footsteps of all Claremont's students on their daily walk into the school.

The young men involved in the national-record winning streak have little left but this monument, personal memories, faded newspaper clippings, and a few grainy sixteen millimeter films to remind them of their remarkable accomplishments. The first athletes who participated in the heyday of Claremont sports are now approaching eighty years of age. Time has taken a toll on their memories, and some have passed away leaving no consolidated history of the glory days. Their story and that of their coach, Bill Welsh, provide a glimpse into small-town high-school sports at a time when such activities dominated South Dakota. Welsh's coaching prowess and his life exhibit the best of sport, of working with young men and women, and of overcoming the trials and tribulations of life, shining the spotlight on six-man football in the state and nation.

A modern-day photograph shows the little-used basketball court. *Marc Rasmussen Collection*

# ONE
## COACH WELSH

# WILLIS ("BILL") WELSH

*For when the One Great Scorer comes*
*to write against your name,*
*He writes—not that you won or lost—*
*but how you played the Game.*
—Grantland Rice, "Alumnus Football"

William Henry Welsh and Katherine Hurley Welsh welcomed the birth of their third child, Willis ("Bill") Welsh, on 14 April 1903, but they knew he would be their last. Tough economic conditions meant that even three children placed a severe burden on the Welsh family. Their older boy, Edmund, was a handsome young man with fair features and a talent for athletics, while Gertrude, their oldest child, had big brown eyes and silky black hair. Edmund ultimately became a successful golfer who operated a highly regarded course in Los Angeles, and Gertrude moved to New York and wrote for the *New York Times*. Their little brother would follow closely in their footsteps, destined for greatness of his own as a coach and as a human being.

Katherine Welsh had suspected that her youngest son Bill was going to be a large child. She gained significantly more weight during her pregnancy than she had for the first two, and she anticipated a difficult labor. Her prediction came true, and despite the forewarning, she found Bill's immense fourteen-pound birth weight a surprise. Typical of the early 1900s, she delivered him at home with the assistance of a midwife.

Bill's father had been born in Stillwater, Minnesota. He, Katherine, and their first two children moved to Aberdeen, South Dakota, at some time between 1898 and 1903. A strapping, handsome young man, William had jet-black hair, a huge handlebar moustache, and a twinkle in his eye that hinted of mischief. Katherine, a thin, attractive woman with dark hair had an intensity about her that she bestowed upon Bill. The Welsh family did not own land or have significant assets, but up until national prohibition caused the company to close, William managed the local distribution office of the John Gund Brewing Company. The job provided a steady source of income and put dinner on the table and clothes on their backs. William and Katherine guided their children well and proved to be great supporters of Bill and his athletic career. However, their marriage suffered once their children left the family home, and although they never divorced, Katherine moved to Spokane, Washington, to live with her sister, and the couple rarely saw each other.

Young Willis Welsh learned to crawl at an early age and walk before friends with similar birthdates. As he entered grade school, he also proved to be faster than his friends and usually found himself picked first for any playground teams. He excelled at competitive sports, where he pushed himself, not content to rest on his considerable natural talent. His work ethic improved his skills and paid off in high-caliber athletic performances. His strong jaw and thick black hair atop a handsome face combined with his prowess at sports to make him a popular kid at school. At the same time, however, he also had a shy streak that only got worse with time. In his high-school annual, his classmates voted him "quickest to blush" and "most bashful." Young Welsh received a lot of good-natured ribbing for this particular quirk, and his friends would keep him in a constant shade of crimson with their good-natured teasing.

By the end of his high-school career, Welsh stood just over five foot eleven inches and weighed 170 pounds. While not large in physical stature, he had an athletic frame built for competition. Had he been more inclined to a social life, he would not have lacked for opportunity, but he was more interested in sports, and Welsh was all business when it came to his athletics. He soon found himself competing above his age group. He excelled in football and basketball, and those who saw him play knew he had the talent to be one of the finest athletes produced in South Dakota.

At the time, Aberdeen was the only major town in the central or northern part of the state. Charles Prior, who ran the Minneapolis office of the Chicago, Milwaukee, & Saint Paul Railroad, had founded Aberdeen just twenty years before Bill Welsh's birth. A railroad town, Aberdeen gained the name "The Hub City" due to its location at the junction of two major railroad systems. Its place as a transportation hub promoted quick population growth, and the community had just over ten thousand residents by 1910. Typical of midwestern towns, Aberdeen lived and died with the fortunes of agriculture and the railroads. The presence of the large storage buildings adjacent to the railroad tracks facilitated commercial farming in the area and provided a means to store grain and reliable transportation to carry farm produce to eastern commodity markets. The combination of local agriculture, its place as a transportation hub, the placement of the county seat, and the fact that the town provided all the services required by the area, all made Aberdeen a thriving and vibrant city.

Welsh attended Sacred Heart Catholic grade and middle school and then went on to Aberdeen Central High School, entering as a sophomore in 1919. The high school provided an educational experience and athletic program superior to any other in a one-hundred-mile radius. The Golden Eagles sports teams were always competitive, and the school offered football, basketball, track, and baseball as varsity sports. The 1919 Aberdeen Central football team had a good nucleus of experienced players, and the varsity squad listed thirty-three young men, including Welsh. In spite of the fact that most of the starters from the previous year's team reported back, Welsh quickly earned a spot on the first team, generally playing halfback and, occasionally, quarterback. He had good speed and ran hard, making him tough to tackle. When the starting quarterback got injured during the 1920 season, Welsh assumed the role and kept that position until he graduated. He also played linebacker on defense, and the coach awarded the "Golden Football" to him in his junior and senior years for making the most open-field tackles. During his senior year, Welsh wore the prized "C" on his uniform denoting his role as captain.

Welsh also achieved an equal degree of success in basketball, and the local community considered him the star player his junior and senior years. His first-year coach in both sports, Rudolph W. Kraushaar, was Welsh's first real mentor in athletics, but Kraushaar resigned at the end of the school year to accept a different position. Because the school district could not find a replacement before the football team started the 1920 season, Welsh and his teammates received instruction from a volunteer coach named Ralph Troga, a former star of the football team at Northern Normal School (now Northern State University), also in Aberdeen. Troga's short-lived mentorship helped develop Welsh's technique as a player and had an impact on his ultimate success. Shortly before the first game of the season, however, D. E. Glasscock joined the staff and took over the coaching duties for the football, basketball, and track teams.

Bill Welsh attended Aberdeen Central High School from 1919 to 1922. *State Archives Collection, South Dakota State Historical Society*

The football team consisted of a group of veteran players and was a physical team with real talent and a strong desire to win. Picking up from where the 1920 team left off, the 1921 Golden Eagles, captained by Welsh, ended the season as conference champions. Welsh's athleticism led to success on the basketball court as well as the gridiron, and he earned varsity letters as a sophomore, junior, and senior. Welsh graduated from high school in the spring of 1922, after contributing to multiple conference and district championships. It was a great start to his athletic career and heralded even better things yet to come.

During his high-school years, Welsh had impressed many fans, but one had been so impressed that he wrote to an associate in Chicago to tell him about the athletic prowess of young Welsh. This associate, a well-funded alumnus of the University of Illinois and a strong advocate of the sports program there, talked to the Illini coach and then contacted the Welsh family to arrange for Bill to visit the campus in the spring of 1922. In the days before the National Collegiate Athletic Association mandated against it, alumni would frequently involve themselves in recruiting great high-school players and pay the cost to get them introduced to the program. For Welsh, it offered a real opportunity, and he was excited at the prospect of playing football at a level he had never imagined possible. His benefactor arranged for a train trip through Chicago and down to the campus in the Urbana-Champaign area. A coach of great renown named Robert ("The Little Dutchman") Zuppke met him there.

Coach Zuppke had achieved legendary status at a relatively young age and would be inducted into the National College Football Hall of Fame in 1951. He had already won two national championships and would win two more before he retired. He attracted talented people to his program, and after meeting Bill Welsh and running him through some exercises, Zuppke was interested in adding the young South Dakotan to his roster. For Welsh, one of the most impressive aspects of the trip involved touring the nearly completed Memorial Stadium named in honor of the brave souls who had fought and died in World War I. The stadium dedication occurred in November 1924 just prior to one of the best college football games in history. In front of a crowd of 66,608 screaming fans, the Fighting Illini defeated the mighty Michigan Wolverines, ending their twenty-game winning streak.

While Welsh toured the campus along with other potential players, he met many of the athletes and coaches, including a freshman on the Illinois team whom the coaches and players held in high regard. Zuppke introduced him as Harold, but Harold asked Bill to call him Red. Zuppke told Welsh that Harold ("Red") Grange would probably crack the starting lineup the following season, and if Welsh accepted the scholarship offer, he would be playing the same position on the team. The coach said Grange would help with Welsh's transition into the Illinois sports program and asked that they pal around during Bill's visit. The two bonded quickly.

Grange, who would go on to a phenomenal career, had nearly skipped the opportunity to play football for fear of injury. He worried that his relatively small stature—he was five foot eleven inches tall but only weighed 170 pounds—might result in severe injury when up against much larger college players. Grange had suffered a head injury in high school that left him unconscious for two days, and even after he regained consciousness, it took a few days before he recovered his ability to speak. The summer before he started his freshman year in college, he had decided to compete for a spot on the basketball and track teams rather than football. Arriving at campus, Grange joined the Zeta Psi Fraternity. When his fraternity brothers, all immense fans of the football team, saw how fast Grange could run, they encouraged him to try out for the football team in spite of his reservations. After much soul searching, he walked in to meet the coach. He knew the squad had already begun practices, and as an unknown, he was a long shot to make the team.

Zuppke, however, saw real potential in Grange and invited him to try out for the team. Putting his fears behind him, Grange began to practice with the freshman team and engaged in drills against the varsity defensive squad. He quickly discovered that his speed and agility more than made up for his size, and when he played as a halfback, the big guys could not hurt what they could not catch. He quickly became the star of the freshman team and dominated the varsity defense for most of that fall's practices. In one scrimmage game, he scored two rushing touchdowns against one of the finest defensive units in the Big Ten Conference.

Thus, in his tour of the campus in 1922, Welsh was introduced to one of the most important players in modern football. At the end of the twentieth century, when various magazines and television networks came out with their "best of" lists for the century, Red Grange was universally voted one of the greatest college football players of all time. In Grange's first collegiate football game his sophomore season, he scored three touchdowns against a strong Nebraska Cornhusker team. In seven games as a sophomore, he ran for 723 yards and scored twelve touchdowns, leading the Illini to an undefeated season and the national championship, the third for Zuppke. During his college career, Grange played in only twenty games but accumulated 2,071 yards in 388 rushing attempts, caught fourteen passes for 253 yards, completed forty of eighty-two passes for 575 yards, and scored thirty-one touchdowns, earning him All-American honors all three years at Illinois. His performance against the Michigan Wolverines in 1924, to open the new Memorial Stadium, really brought him to national prominence and placed the eyes of the nation on the Illinois football program.

Undefeated, and gunning for a national championship, the Michigan Wolverines met the Fighting Illini in Urbana-Champaign, Illinois, that year. Promoted as the best football team of the decade, the Wolverines looked unbeatable, but on the opening kickoff, Grange ran the ball back for ninety-five yards and a touchdown, following it with three more long touchdown runs in the first twelve minutes. This offensive production in the first quarter equaled the total touchdowns scored against Michigan over the previous two seasons. By the end of the game, Grange had run for another score and passed for a sixth. Behind Grange's thirty-six points, Illinois ended the Wolverines' twenty-game winning streak and their national title hopes, 39 to 14. That historic performance earned Grange the nickname "The Galloping Ghost," a moniker he would carry for the remainder of his college career and into the new National Football League.

Following his visit to the campus and his favorable interactions with the players and coaches, Welsh, having impressed Zuppke with his toughness, committed to play for the University of Illinois starting in the fall of 1923. It was rare for an athlete from the Dakotas to find his way into a major college football program, and Welsh's family and the community took pride in the announcement of his decision to attend Illinois. They organized a celebration preceding his long train trip to college. Dozens of his friends, family, and members of the community attended the going-away party, a display that made the shy Welsh a bit uncomfortable. While used to winning and holding high expectations for his own performance, he had not yet realized how the people around him shared in the opportunity he had been given to play for the Fighting Illini. For the first time, he observed the impact a great player had on a small community and, in turn, the community on the player. This opportunity was not exclusively his experience; rather, it was an experience shared by the town's residents, and when he stepped onto the train, they came with him in spirit.

Welsh arrived at the Urbana-Champaign campus in early August 1923 and enrolled as a general studies student. The college town is almost nine hundred miles from Aberdeen. Given the relatively slow nature of train travel in the 1920s and the late summer heat, Welsh likely arrived hot and tired, but he had no time to dwell on his journey. A scholarship athlete, he had to race to the practice field before he could even unpack. By rule at the time, the university did not allow freshmen to play varsity football, and all first-year students played instead on the freshman club, which mimicked the offense and defense of the team the varsity would be playing the upcoming weekend. As a result, the freshmen always competed against a powerful Big Ten team—their own. Over one hundred fifty athletes showed up for the first practice, hoping for a shot at playing for Bob Zuppke's team, and Welsh discovered that he never had to work so hard for anything in his life. The athletes at Illinois were bigger, faster, and more intense than any he had faced in high school, but Welsh held his own and earned a spot on the roster.

Players in football's early years suffered far more injuries and played a much more dangerous game than at any other time in history. In 1909, for instance, a reported twenty-six players died while involved in the game at all levels. The game was getting faster and more sophisticated, but the safety equipment the players used had not kept pace and rarely prevented injury. The players wore helmets made of leather with limited padding and no facemask. Prior to the 1920s, the game depended heavily on running the ball to advance it, and contact consisted largely of pushing as opposed to impact tackles. However, as the sport evolved, the passing game became more prevalent and put increasing numbers of young men at risk, as a full running start prior to contact often resulted in a more dangerous collision. By 1923, the prevalence of concussions, broken bones, and spinal injuries was as high as it had been since the elimination of mass-formation plays in the late 1800s.

In spite of the risks, Welsh worked hard to become the best football player he could possibly be in one of the top programs in the country. As the coaching staff observed his skill during the pre-season, he earned more and more attention at practice. The coaches played him at running back and linebacker for the freshman team, and Zuppke considered him a candidate for a starting role on the varsity teams in the 1924 season. Because he and Grange played the same position, Welsh spent a lot of time working closely with the older player as they sought to improve their skills as runners. Zuppke and his coaching staff embraced innovation, and Zuppke's style would influence Welsh in his career as both player and coach. Welsh was a motivated, happy person who had the whole world at his feet. However, optimism and opportunity cannot prevent injury, and he had no way of anticipating what would happen next.

The first real setback of Welsh's life caused a change in the direction of his football career. During a practice just before the first game of his freshman season, while playing on the defensive side of the ball, Welsh pursued an offensive player who had broken away from the pack on the opposite side of the field. With his great speed, he picked a perfect angle to close on the player for the tackle. Approaching at a dead run, he suddenly felt a horrible pain in his eye. As he reached up to find out what happened, he found a piece of metal from the cleat of the offensive player had lodged in his eyeball. Emergency personnel rushed Welsh to the local hospital. As the doctor completed his examination, he told Welsh that he could save his eye, but it would require a series of complex and expensive surgeries. At this point in his life, Welsh had no insurance or personal resources to pay for such extraordinary care. The young South Dakotan suddenly understood that he stood a serious chance of losing an eye, which would certainly end his football career.

When word spread about the injury and his predicament of not having the money for surgery, the same person who had paid for Welsh's trip to Illinois offered to pay for the medical costs. Welsh was relieved that he would retain his vision, but he chafed at his inability to participate in practices until the eye healed. As he endured the painful surgeries, Welsh promised himself he would find a way to return to the playing field. Upon release from the hospital, he made certain to attend each practice even though he could not officially participate. He kept his place on the team and maintained his conditioning in the hope that he might return before the end of the season. Unfortunately, he did not heal in time, but stood on the sideline as the team went on to win the school's third national championship in 1923.

The eye injury eventually healed, but just a few months later, in the spring of 1924, Welsh faced a significantly more dangerous medical emergency. In April, his appendix ruptured, an often fatal condition at the time due to the infections the rupture could cause in the bowels. Welsh spent weeks in the hospital but finally beat the infection and returned to class to finish the school year at Illinois. The combination of the eye injury followed by the ruptured appendix forced Welsh to make a tough decision. Since he had lost his opportunity to play on the team, he could no longer hold a scholarship. Unable to afford the school based on his own resources, Welsh returned to his hometown of Aberdeen to examine his future. Although disappointed at the turn of events, he decided he wanted to continue his schooling.

Welsh consulted with friends and family over how he should proceed. After looking at his alternatives, he chose to reenter

This postcard shows a building on the Northern Normal College campus. *State Archives Collection, South Dakota State Historical Society*

college at Northern Normal College, located down the street from his childhood home. After transferring, he quickly won spots playing both football and basketball for the Wolves. At Northern, he once again played running back, and no longer competing with Big-Ten-caliber players, he achieved immediate success. In 1925, Welsh starred on the South Dakota Intercollegiate Conference (SDIC) championship football team, coached by Jacob Speelman. He also played basketball that year and enjoyed a good season both personally and as part of a successful team. The Wolves ended the year with an overall record of nine wins and five losses and a tied conference record, placing them in the middle of the SDIC pack. In the following years, due to injury problems, Welsh focused on football only; the 1925–1926 basketball season represented the end of his college basketball career. Because of the injuries at Illinois, Welsh came to Northern with four years of eligibility remaining. He competed for the football team all four years and, in his final two years, captained the team and was named most-valuable player. The 1928 season was his last as a football player. Due to the state of his finances, he took the next year off to work before returning to finish his degree.

Welsh's path to a diploma took longer than anticipated, but he demonstrated the persistence that would carry him through many challenges to come. Upon graduation, he looked forward to a career as a teacher, and for the first time, the idea of coaching sports began to appeal to him, as well. Having seen coaches such as Bob Zuppke in action, Welsh determined to study all aspects of the sports he would coach. He knew that just because he had been a great player he would not automatically be a great coach. Rather, the most successful coach was the man who best understood the nature of the athletes and the rules of the game. The Illinois influence combined with his time at Northern Normal shaped his approach to the game. Coaching was more than just teaching the fundamentals. Innovation on the field and promotion off of it were as important as wins when it came to filling the seats with spectators, and more spectators meant more resources available to support his teams. Welsh had learned these lessons through observation. One of the intangible benefits of his injury at Illinois had been the opportunity to observe the art of coaching football from the sidelines. Coach Zuppke had taught Welsh the importance of staying ahead of the innovation curve. He taught him to embrace the rulebook in order to know all that was possible within the rules of the game. As a result, Welsh found he could push the margins of the game because he understood the dimensions of these margins better than anyone else did. His college football career had not turned out as planned, but it shaped his future high-school sports programs and contributed to his future success in a significant way.

Another event at Northern also shaped Welsh's future. Shaking off some of the shyness that had plagued him earlier in life, Welsh sampled the social aspects of college life as fully as his athletic and academic pursuits allowed. During those social forays, Welsh met a young student enrolled in the nursing program at Saint Luke's Hospital in Aberdeen. Her name was Edna Mattson, and she came from Terraville in the Black Hills of South Dakota. She was the daughter of two Finnish immigrants and the second oldest of eight children. Her parents had come to the state to find their fortunes in the gold towns of Lead and Deadwood. As the surface gold became scarce, Mattson's father took a job as a miner in the Homestake Gold Mine, while her mother worked in one of the local hotels as a janitor. Her parents placed great importance on the value of education, and Mattson was an exceptional student. Finishing her high-school education early, she lied about her age to gain entrance into the Saint Luke's Hospital nursing program. At the age of sixteen, she moved to Aberdeen and began her higher education.

A couple of years later, Bill Welsh met Edna Mattson, whose good looks complemented her adventurous streak. The couple enjoyed each other's company and soon became inseparable.

In 1929, Welsh asked her to marry him, but as graduation approached, the couple experienced some rocky moments that resulted in their breaking up. Each held a different dream for their lives, and although much in love, they chose, amicably, to go their separate ways.

Once she had qualified as a nurse, the adventurous Mattson traveled to California to experience a different culture. Her nursing skills kept her employed, and her travels took her to the epicenter of the entertainment world when she settled in the Los Angeles area. There she met the actress Julie Haydon, who hired her as a private nurse and traveling companion. Haydon had come to California from Illinois in the late 1920s seeking fame and fortune and had captured the eye of the talent scouts. She starred in a number of successful films and worked with some of the major stars of the era. When Mattson joined Haydon, the actor was on the cusp of some big roles in movies such as *Age of Innocence* (1934) and *The Scoundrel* (1935), in which she starred alongside Noel Coward. In 1935, the two women traveled to New York, where Haydon was to star in Philip Barry's Broadway production of *Bright Star*. The cross-country train trip took Mattson through Aberdeen, offering an opportunity for a brief stop. Mattson phoned Welsh to tell him of her plans, and they met while the entourage rested at the station. Mattson then continued on to New York and Welsh returned to his new coaching job in Kimball, South Dakota, but their romance had been rekindled.

While Mattson had finished her nursing degree and headed to California, Welsh completed his college education in the spring of 1930, just a few months after the stock-market crash of 1929, which signaled more than a decade of economic depression. Through his connections with alumni of Northern Normal in Aberdeen, Bill learned of a coaching job in Kimball, South Dakota, a small town about one hundred fifty miles south of Aberdeen. Jobs were scarce at that time, and he jumped at the opportunity to put his name into the hat of potential candidates. The Kimball superintendent contacted him, and they met for an interview. The superintendent found Welsh's intensity and eagerness impressive, reasoning that the students would follow a coach who had already proven his skill as a college star. After the interview, he made Welsh an offer that was accepted on the spot, and Bill Welsh, the athlete, became Bill Welsh, the coach.

Welsh knew he was fortunate to find employment right away, and it was in no small part due to the regional fame he had achieved as a player. His wage at Kimball would not make him wealthy, but he would be able to live a comfortable life, and he would be doing what he loved. Welsh brought his exceptional character and tremendous work ethic to Kimball, where he faced challenges with confidence and moral fortitude, modeling the behavior he expected from his students. Coach Welsh was quintessentially professional, and to see him without a jacket and tie was a rarity. As a born leader, he squeezed the maximum performance from his athletes, and his commitment to honor and integrity influenced anyone he mentored.

When Welsh arrived in Kimball in the fall of 1930, the town had a population of about eleven hundred people. Located on South Dakota Highway 45 in Brule County just twenty miles southeast of Chamberlain, Kimball had an agricultural-based economy, with various diverse service-related businesses, manufacturers, and retail stores. The residents were proud of their little town, and despite the failing national economy, most found a way to make a living. Elmer's Barbershop formed the hub of male culture, the place in which the men went to chat about recent happenings around town. For a reasonable price, a customer received a fine shave and haircut, and he threw in jokes and opinions for free. Welsh learned just how valuable the barber's opinions were when he went for his first haircut. The trim came with a player-by-player breakdown of all the athletes he had inherited with the coaching job. The town barber was a wealth of information, not just about the Kimball Ki-Otes, but also about all the teams in the Custer Battlefield Highway (CBH) Conference (Gann Valley, White Lake, Chamberlain, Plankinton, Mount Vernon, Pukwana, Hopper, and Stickney). The new coach discovered that he had inherited an eager group of athletes and that he had the ingredients for a successful sports program. The names of the boys who would likely form Welsh's first Kimball squad revealed a hodgepodge of nationalities: Duba, Crocket, Williamson, Hrdina, Brady, Donner, Stowell, Houda, Lynn, and Foltz. The parents and grandparents of these boys had traveled to Kimball from Europe and the eastern United States during the previous four decades. Those early settlers sought a new start, hoping for brighter futures in South Dakota than those they foresaw in Germany, Czechoslovakia, Norway, or Ireland. When the new coach met the players just before the start of the 1930–1931 school year, he discovered that the barber had it right. Kimball really did have some good athletes with a lot of potential.

Kimball High School offered the sports common to small towns in the area—football, basketball, track, and baseball—

and Welsh would coach each team. He started this first assignment with excitement and enthusiasm. Assessing the potential, Welsh expected to put some competitive basketball and track teams together and hoped he might squeeze some wins from the football teams. Because of the size of the community and a limited enrollment in the school, however, the football program struggled to field enough boys each year to put together a competitive eleven-man football team. This situation, which confronted most small schools in the state, plagued Welsh during his years at Kimball. He always got the most out of those who went out for football, but in some seasons, his teams consisted of no more than sixteen players. In 1933, Welsh would be surprised when thirty boys turned out for the opening day of practice. He had enough boys for a full scrimmage with subs, but when he scanned the group, he realized that not a single player weighed more than one hundred fifty pounds.

The challenges would be many, and Welsh's initial football team in 1930 lost more games than it won. In the years before a wide-open offense dominated the sport, games often ended as low-scoring affairs, with ties common. The 1931 football team, for instance, ended with a record of two wins, two losses, and three ties. However, he counted one of the ties as a moral vic-

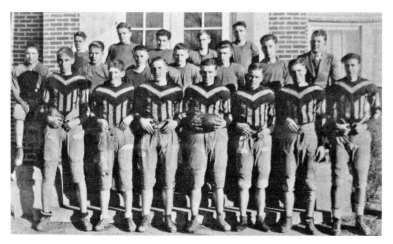

Bill Welsh, middle row, at right, coached the Kimball Ki-Otes football squad, shown here in 1934. *Welsh Family Collection*

tory and a sign of progress for the program. The Ki-Otes played a powerful Chamberlain team to a tie that year, and the Kimball faithful knew that any year in which Chamberlain did not beat them in football was a good year. Still, given the challenges, Welsh would be unable to put together a championship-caliber football squad during his tenure in Kimball.

Welsh's basketball teams, however, enjoyed more success and never finished lower than third place in the conference. His 1931 team even challenged for the District 24 title. But Kimball still measured itself against Chamberlain, to whom they lost that year in the district finals. It seemed that the Chamberlain Cubs forever had Kimball's number, and losing to them had become a theme repeated too often for the Kimball faithful's taste. Between 1928 and the spring of 1931, Kimball had not defeated Chamberlain in any sporting contest, and the fans and players had become a bit sensitive to the attitude of the Chamberlain fans and players. In 1932, the Ki-Otes finally broke through and won the CBH Conference basketball title, followed by their first district basketball championship under Welsh. The 1932 district track title followed the basketball title, and Kimball won the District 24 basketball title again in 1934–1935, after being runner-up to Stickney the previous year. Welsh had brought success on the sports field to this small town in a big way.

Going into the 1935–1936 season, Kimball fans confidently expected the basketball team to dominate the league, but the squad caused a stir when they lost the first two games of the season. The fans' discomfort did not last long, for the team went on to an unbeaten stretch of thirteen games to finish the regular season. Although the team lost the conference title to Pukwana, it managed to win the District 24 title. In the opening game of the 1935 regionals at Salem, Kimball played nearby Marion. The two schools had a real battle that left them tied with just thirty-seven seconds left. After Welsh called a time-out, Kimball missed two shots, and there were two held balls. At the end of the game, Marion scored on a long shot, and the crowd rushed the court. No final whistle was heard, and the official timer said time had expired while the shot was in the air. The crowd and players from Kimball were certain that the shot should not count, and, with that controversy hanging over the ending, the referee declared Marion the winner by a final score of 25 to 23. The next evening, Kimball won the consolation crown over Letcher, 47 to 35.

Fred Houda, a member of the Ki-Otes at the time, indicated that the loss was set up when Welsh received a technical foul after stepping on the line of the coach's box. The referee was rumored to have a Marion bias. When Marion made both foul shots, tying the score and setting up the controversial ending, the Kimball fans insisted that the referee had railroaded their team. Welsh, however, remained calm and professional. A technical foul on him was nearly unheard of, for he had been well trained to remain in control of his emotions, and he insisted on the same from his players. The call would be a sore point between the communities for years. Welsh refused to add fuel to the fire and did not mention it again after the event, but if someone at Elmer's Barbershop were asked about the game, they would be happy to provide an in-depth analysis of the events, seasoned with some salty words of disgust.

In his seven years at Kimball, Welsh contributed significantly to the town's sports history. He also helped townspeople discover their role in the success of the high-school program. He made the game entertaining and showed the boys what it meant to be a part of a winning team. Foregoing some of the traditional basketball styles, he favored more aggressive approaches, which resulted in more wins and more excitement. Woody Wentzy, a Kimball journalist, noted in a 1932 article that he was amazed at how much faster the boys played under the young coach.

The time Welsh had spent at Illinois had affected his approach to coaching. The excitement and interest generated around the football program there had mesmerized him, and he soaked up all he could. While he was not likely to coach in front of sixty-thousand screaming fans, the principles underlying the Fighting Illini's success could work at smaller programs, he reasoned. Welsh became convinced that a small-town team could achieve greatness, but it would require the entire community, not just the players, to become champions. The members of Kimball had to be coached into understanding that winning was an attitude and that top teams came from a community tolerating nothing less than the best. Once fully engaged in its support for the team, the town would inspire the players with its excitement. The actual techniques of the game were only part of the program; it took a community's dedication to winning to provide the needed spark to enable their youngsters to achieve success.

Once the community threw its support behind the team, Welsh could get on with coaching the athletes, which was much more than giving instruction on the proper execution of plays. Welsh understood the importance of psychology and the mental aspects of the game, and with his natural intelligence and communication skills, he became a master of motivation. He began by assessing his team's talent, identifying the players with the greatest potential and offering them a chance to compete at the highest level they could manage. Age was not a barrier, and as they earned it, youngsters received a chance to prove their skills against older players. The boys quickly learned that more effort equaled more playing time. Those who worked the hardest would start the game, which meant each player had to earn his starting position in practice during the week. This ethos played a major role in the team's successes. It also developed the skills of talented young players quickly because they did not have to wait until they were a certain age. Once he had discovered and motivated the potential talents within his program, Welsh taught the fundamentals of the sport relentlessly. He made sure the boys drilled until they became experts in each of the skills they needed to compete. Such an emphasis on fundamentals meant that the boys instinctively knew the right thing to do; they just sensed it, rather than thought about it.

Having chosen to coach at a small school, Welsh insisted that his athletes be involved in every sport available. Borrowing from his own experiences, he instituted a consistent and thorough set of drills, reasoning that repetition would lead to perfection in execution, that physical exercise would create endurance and strength, and that exposure to sports on a year-round basis would keep the athletes' skill sets sharp. As the boys developed their own abilities, they also learned team play and came to understand the roles inherent in each position on the team. Welsh then matched them to a role and molded their lessons to include the expectations of that role. If properly coached, a player could step onto the field or the basketball court and plug into the game seamlessly without the rest of the team needing to adjust.

The short time at Illinois had also taught Welsh the lesson that a successful coach was bigger than life, someone who possessed the promotional skills of circus legend P. T. Barnum, the football skills of Knute Rockne, and the personality of Will Rogers. Welsh had also learned the lessons of football as a game and as a business. Sport was entertainment, and to put together the best show took more than just winning. Without adequate resources, it was impossible to build a sports program capable of achieving greatness. In theory, successful sports programs would be self-funding and would be able to bring resources to the school in excess of cost. He also understood the effect a high-school team could have on the residents of the town; a town united around its sports program was a town capable of forgetting the hardships of life for a few hours a week. Welsh possessed a knack for creating excitement and, early on, discovered the advantages of giving townspeople a sense of inclusion. He never had difficulty gaining support for his teams either financially or through donated labor. Those asked would come up with the time or resources needed because they considered themselves as much a part of the team as the players. Whether they wore the uniform or played in the game was irrelevant; each had a role to play that contributed to the outcome.

During those seven years in Kimball, Bill Welsh represented a breath of fresh air to a small town suffering the effects of the Great Depression. His efforts helped the town maintain a sense of itself in the face of adversity. Welsh's leadership helped to keep spirits elevated. He turned the games he coached into spectacles and even added the first homecoming celebration for Kimball High School. The concept of homecoming was a recent development in that part of the state, and by introducing it, Welsh effectively increased the level of pride the students and athletes felt about their school. But even though the coach poured his energy and talents into the high school and his students, he found himself lonely for Edna Mattson.

Welsh had rediscovered his feelings for Mattson when she had stopped to see him while accompanying Julie Haydon on her 1935 trip across the country. When he finished teaching classes that Friday, he had traveled to Aberdeen to meet her at the train station. They rushed to embrace each other, and when the time came to leave, neither wanted to let go. As the train traveled on to Minneapolis and then New York, it became clear to Mattson that she belonged with Welsh. While staying with Haydon and her entourage in one of the finest hotels in Manhattan, the young nurse received a phone call. As she lifted the receiver, she heard a familiar voice on the other end. Summoning all his courage, Welsh asked her, one more time, to be his wife. For the second time, Mattson said yes, and when Haydon's play closed after only ten performances, Mattson hopped on the next train back to South Dakota. In following this path, Mattson left behind the excitement of Hollywood, the glitter of the Great White Way, and an anticipated trip to Europe for a more sedate and challenging lifestyle in the small-town Midwest.

On the train ride across the plains, Mattson pondered her

return to her fiancé. Having associated with the leaders of dramatic society for a number of years, she knew how to make a grand entrance, and that is exactly what she did. In Manhattan, just before she boarded the train, she visited some of the finest women's clothing shops and purchased a beautiful dress. To accessorize, she added a large brimmed black hat, long black gloves, some stunning high heels, and jewelry given to her by Julie Haydon as a thank you for her friendship. As Mattson approached her destination, she donned this finery, checked her image in the mirror, and smiled. Stepping off the train, she asked the local ticket agent where she might find Coach Welsh. He said there was a basketball tournament going on at the high school, and the coach was likely there. Mattson entered the gym mid-play, directly across the court from where Welsh sat on the team bench. Without thinking anything of it, she strutted across the playing surface and into the arms of a surprised coach. Play stopped, and the crowd, understanding the meaning of her arrival, stood and clapped as the two embraced.

Welsh and Mattson married in Kimball in July 1935. Financial considerations forced the new couple to set up their first home in a local eight-room hotel. As a home, it was tiny, but at this point in their lives, the space proved sufficient. A few months later, the young wife surprised her husband with the news that she was pregnant. A curly-haired tyke with big eyes and an infectious smile, Jane Katherine Welsh was soon the apple of her daddy's eye. With a wife and a baby, Welsh's reliance on Elmer's Barbershop took a different tack. The coach discovered that the towels used to soothe the faces of customers prior to a shave made exceptional diapers, and little Jane's bottom was thereafter covered by towel's from the barbershop, a great example of community support for its coach.

In Jane's first year, a near tragedy occurred when a fire erupted in the hotel. As smoke filled the room, the baby began to cough. The noise woke her mother, who had just dozed off. Because of this tiny girl's warning, Edna Welsh managed to get her daughter out of the building and alert the rest of the residents. Every-one got out safely while the hotel burned to the ground. In the local paper, Jane received credit for saving a number of lives that night with her coughs. Welsh was at the gym at the time, coaching a basketball game. When a neighbor came running into the building to let folks know the hotel was on fire, Welsh jumped up from the bench, grabbed the game-clock from the scorer's table, and ran to the building to make certain of his family's safety. When everyone was secure, someone asked the coach why he was carrying the clock from the gym. "I knew they could not finish the game without a clock," he said, "and I wanted to make sure we did not have to forfeit." He returned to the gym after the fire, and Kimball won the game.

After seven somewhat successful years in Kimball, Welsh learned of a coaching position at Webster, in the northeastern part of South Dakota. With a population of approximately two thousand, Webster was a larger community located forty-five miles east of Aberdeen. Webster's sports program had a long history of accomplishment, and this legacy of winning attracted Welsh at this stage of his career. The Webster superintendent, R. J. Strand, contacted Welsh and asked him if he would inter-view for the position. The job contained the elements Welsh had found missing in the Kimball program, and when the su-perintendent offered him the position, he accepted. At the end of the school year, the Welsh family packed its belongings and headed north to a new town and new responsibility.

The Webster job gave the family more income and provided a student population adequate to field a competitive football team. On the personal side, Webster's thriving community was a great place to raise a little girl, and he and Edna looked for-ward to having more children. As in Kimball, agriculture drove the Webster economy, but the railroad also provided additional jobs and had a positive effect on local property. The proximity of Webster to his homctown allowed Welsh and his family to interact with his extended family and with friends from their

youth. The area also offered great fishing and hunting opportunities, and Bill looked forward to catching northern pike,
small-mouth bass, and walleye.

Webster had established itself as a sports town, and its
teams had been the league champions in football, basketball,
and track the previous three years leading up to Welsh's arrival.
However, the spring prior to his entrance as coach, the school
graduated eleven of its key players, and Welsh now worried that
the cupboard might be bare. Instead, he discovered that the
town had a sports program that created quality players year
after year, and he had eager and capable underclassmen ready
to step into the starting roles on each team. In fact, 1937 was
his best year at Webster, with all his teams doing well. The football team provided his first winning season as a high-school
football coach. The varsity squad had twenty-two players, and
the Bearcats ended the year with four wins and one loss in conference play, and six wins and two losses overall, holding the
opposition scoreless in five of those victories. This record was
good enough for a runner-up finish in conference play. The
only losses came at the hands of Sisseton, their archrival, and
the much larger Watertown squad. Welsh finally had a football
program with enough players to allow him to apply his coaching skills without having to revert to survival mode every time
the team suffered an injury. He could now fully utilize what he

The 1937
Webster
Welshmen
football team
poses for
its annual
photograph
with Welsh
standing
on the left.
*Welsh Family
Collection*

had learned during his days at Illinois, Northern State, and as the coach of the Kimball Ki-Otes, and the players responded to his lessons.

The first football season was followed by the 1938 Northeast Conference (NEC) title in basketball and the NEC District basketball championship. The track team won the 1938 NEC track title in Milbank by scoring 47.5 points in a hard-fought contest, and the same group took second place in the regional track meet held in Aberdeen and even earned points at the state tournament. Later that summer, Welsh earned his first state title when the Webster baseball team won the South Dakota State Amateur Baseball championship. Along the way, they enjoyed an undefeated season, culminating in a defeat of the Aberdeen team for the state title. The team averaged eleven runs a game and held their opponents to an average of three runs.

The accomplishments of Welsh's first year were even more exciting given the quality of the competition. The NEC had a reputation for fielding some of the most competitive teams in the state from relatively small towns. The conference at the time included Webster (population 2,033), Sisseton (1,840), Milbank (2,549), Britton (1,473), Doland (538), Redfield (2,573), Groton (1,036), and Clark (1,372). The rivalries were many, and each team had a substantial following of fans willing to brave the challenging weather in support of their boys. The seats were full at most games, and the crowd inspired the players; the fans' excitement was contagious, and the swell of energy pushed the boys to succeed. For Welsh, a game in the NEC actually resembled those he had experienced during his high-school and college days, and he enjoyed the move to a bigger program.

But 1938 resonated with Welsh on a far more important level, as well; he and Edna had added a son to their family. With the birth of Jean Raymond, Welsh threw himself into being the best role model he could be for his son, and from the first day, he was sure that the boy would be a football star. Welsh called

Jean "Brother," or his "Little Assistant Coach," and Jean was always interested in anything involving his father.

Welsh spent seven years in Webster, and while the faces changed on his teams, the names remained the same: Hagen, Burns, Koenig, Thomas, Watters, Storsteen, Blocker, Monshaugen, Bartos, Hesla, Aslesen, Bloom, Fick, Gruba, Skoba, Kaiser, Slattery, Smith, Paulson, Johnson, Schmidt, Brostad, Mickelsen, Estwick, Dougherty, Stewart, Harding, Overton, Fickler, Mahlen, Stewart, Hallstrom, Geis, Sauer, Flattum, Syverson, and Christianson. The ethnic mix leaned toward German and Scandinavian populations with a touch of Slavic thrown in for flavor. The boys were tough, strong, and had the competi-

Edna
Mattson
Welsh with
Jane (right)
and Jean
(left). *Welsh
Family
Collection*

tive spirit needed for championship sports programs. Welsh brought high expectations with him, and his teams matched his desire to be the best. With the graduation of Kenneth Storsteen at the end of the 1938–1939 school year, Webster's star athlete in Welsh's first season, the coach had to rebuild the team in his second year. Fortunately, Welsh managed to find the right mix of players, and the team finished second in the NEC again with a record of four wins, three losses, and a tie. The basketball team, however, struggled, winning eleven and losing thirteen, but his track team took second in the NEC and second in the regional meet in Aberdeen, making, once again, for a successful year.

Over the next couple of years, Welsh's Webster teams maintained decent records, but in 1941–1942, the athletic teams went through a tough spell, lacking sufficient talent for even Welsh's coaching skills to coax out many wins. That one season, though, represented the low point of Welsh's tenure in Webster. The following year, the football team had its best year since Welsh had arrived, winning five, with just a single loss and a single tie. Webster was the co-champion of the NEC that year with Milbank. Matching the success of the football squad, the basketball team won thirteen, lost two, and won the NEC championship, before losing to Britton in the district tournament held in Langford. The track team again took second in the NEC championship—still not quite able to break that particular glass ceiling—and third in the regional meet. This group of athletes set five school records and allowed Welsh to set the foundations for what would become a track-and-field dynasty over the next decade in Webster.

The success Welsh had in Webster proved to be the cornerstone of his National High School Athletic Coaches Association Hall of Fame career. The true measure of his success lay in his achievements across all the sports offered by Webster High School. He also revamped the athletic club for the varsity players. The W Club recognized key accomplishments, built a sense of camaraderie, and promoted the idea that being a varsity athlete meant something special. Welsh improved the club, making it far more important than it had previously been. Even after Welsh left Webster for his next assignment, the program he had so powerfully influenced continued to enjoy success on the court, track, and field. The 1945 Webster basketball team won the NEC title, district championship, regional championship, and finished second in the State B tournament. The following three years, the Bearcats won the State B basketball title each year. It was an amazing run by some talented boys, and it paid tribute to the program Bill Welsh had installed in the town.

Welsh's success in Webster boosted his reputation as a coach, and his stock was rising in high-school coaching circles. But with the birth of his third child, Judy Anne, in early 1943, Welsh

(left) Bill Welsh at Webster High School.
*Welsh Family Collection*

(right) Jane, Judy Anne, and "Brother."
*Welsh Family Collection*

suddenly had a family of five with just a coach's pay to support them, leaving the family feeling the financial limitations of his career choice. Bill and Edna decided that they needed to figure out a way to improve their situation. Through his contacts in coaching, Bill received a call from the superintendent of schools in Forest City, Iowa. He wanted Welsh to take over the sports program at the high school there. The financial package offered was a nice improvement, and the athletic program he would inherit was exceptional. After reviewing the offer, the Welshes accepted the posting and packed up their lives for the move to northern Iowa.

**3** The Welsh family arrived in Forest City, Iowa, on the first of September 1943. Bill assumed the position of head coach at the high school and took on responsibility for the varsity sports of football, basketball, track, and baseball. Forest City, located in the north-central part of the state in Winnebago County, was a bigger community than either Webster or Kimball, and it had an exceptional history of sports success. As elsewhere in the Midwest, Scandinavians and Germans made up much of the population of Forest City. It was not exactly a tourist destination, but Lake Okoboji, a beautiful summer playground, could be reached within three hours, and in the 1930s, the Civilian Conservation Corps had built an intriguing stone observation tower at Pilot Knob State Park, just outside the city. Reverend C. S. Salveson, the pastor of Immanuel Lutheran Church, had founded Waldorf Community College in 1903, giving the town an institution of higher education. Forest City fit Bill Welsh's idea of a great town and offered him an even better platform on which to practice his coaching arts.

Welsh inherited a sports program with a tradition of winning. The teams from Forest City were always competitive, having accumulated many championships over the years, and Forest City meant dynasty to those who opposed them in any athletic event. Talented athletes abounded, and the boys in the program expected to be among the best teams in the conference year after year. The school had already achieved much of what Welsh hoped to create in a high-school sports program; he merely had to continue that tradition, which he did. Welsh picked up the baton from his predecessor with alacrity, and his first football team went undefeated, winning the 1943 North

Iowa Conference football championship. The Forest City Indians dominated its competition and outscored its opponents by 186 to 30 points.

The move to Iowa forced Bill and Edna to adjust to a new home a long way from their family and friends in South Dakota. Unfamiliar with the new community, they kept busy with their children, and Bill focused on his teams. By that time Jean Welsh was five years old, and his interest in sports had grown. He was an enthusiastic little boy who always seemed to have a ball in his hands and a smile on his face. As he grew older, he spent more and more time with his father and he began to interact with Welsh's players at practices, where he became the team mascot, greatly amusing players and fans alike.

Life seemed to be working out quite well for the Welshes, but as Bill had discovered on the practice field in Illinois, life is seldom fair, and when things seem to be going best, life sometimes knocks a person to his knees. An unremarkable Saturday dawned on 4 December 1943, and Welsh agreed to help his friend Ben Anderson move furniture to his new home just outside Forest City. Bill took his son along, for Jean was keen to play with his friend Jon, Ben's son. When they arrived at the Anderson home, Bill started moving furniture, and Jean joined Jon and another friend, four-year-old Carol Sue Johnson, on the swings in her backyard, just across the street. The children played for half an hour on the swings and in the sand box and

Smiling, Welsh (back row, left) stands with his Forest City Indians in preparation for the 1943 season. *Welsh Family Collection*

then wandered over to some tennis courts located across the alley from the Johnson home. After playing for a while, the children decided to return to the Andersons'. As children often do with no consequence, Jean stepped off the curb and into the street without looking. But he stepped right into the path of a car driven by John Hutchen of nearby Thompson.

Hutchen and his wife and family had just said goodbye to their son who had been home on leave and had left to ship out to the war. Hutchen suffered from poor vision and should not have been driving that day, but he had taken the chance in order to see his boy off. As he drove down the street headed

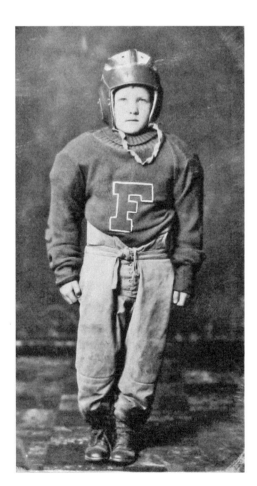

Jean ("Brother") Welsh
served as team mascot for
the Forest City Indians.
*Welsh Family Collection*

for home, Hutchen simply did not see Jean and, even after the impact, continued down the street without realizing what had happened, until he looked back to see Jean lying prone in the street. The small boy died that day of a skull fracture, and the only witness to the accident was Jean's young friend, Jon. Welsh, who had been delivering furniture to Andersdon's new place, returned to find the tragedy had already unfolded. The local police and the Lutheran minister, Reverend Reinertson, met Welsh at the scene. In seconds, his seemingly wonderful life fell apart; the situation was made so much worse by knowing that he had to tell Edna the news. Nothing had prepared him for this event. It was the darkest day in his life, and it would haunt him the rest of his days.

Bill and Edna buried their son in the cemetery just outside Forest City. They had decided on that spot even though doing so meant Jean would be left alone in a strange place if the Welshes ever decided to leave. They reached the difficult decision with heavy hearts because neither one believed the family would stay in the community for the rest of Bill's career. With the untimely death of their beloved Brother, their hearts told them it would be too hard to remain so near the site of the accident. Jean's death had a profound impact on their lives. In time, the Welsh family returned to a place of normalcy, but it was a bumpy road for many years.

To compound matters, after the funeral, Edna's health began to deteriorate. She had been consistently suffering from a cold, which soon turned into pneumonia and, with the emotional stress tied to the death of her son, ultimately caused damage to the lining of her lungs. The grief combined with the virus to overwhelm her body. Local doctors offered her little help; they lacked the ability to diagnose Edna's illness and, even if they had been able to do so, they lacked the facilities to treat the problem. Bill watched his wife fade more by the day and knew he had to do something quickly. He decided to take her to Rochester, Minnesota, where better medical resources could be found. With the help of the local doctor, Bill wrapped Edna in ice to reduce the hemorrhaging and drove her straight through to what is now the Mayo Clinic. After a series of tests, the doctors found that damage from the pneumonia was causing bleeding in her lungs, and the doctors advised Bill that the situation was potentially life threatening.

Over the next year, Edna spent more time in the hospital than at home. A few months after Jean's death, and after she had gone home, her doctors discovered that she was pregnant, a dangerous situation for Edna, who still suffered from bleeding in her lungs. Her doctors advised that she remain in the hospital until the baby was born, which she did. At the end of this medical ordeal, when Edna returned home with their newborn daughter, Jean Patsy ("Patty"), her weight had fallen to eighty-five pounds, but the happy little girl she bore in her arms made the bed rest worth it. The birth of Patty did not cure the sorrow, but their daughter's sweet demeanor and gentle nature helped Bill and Edna move forward.

Bill now had three little girls who needed their father. He had a wife who suffered from a grave medical condition and a job and responsibilities that he needed to fulfill. There were bills to pay, a family to feed, and games to win. Welsh's upbringing and the midwestern society in which he lived meant that he found it hard to show his emotions; he kept them tightly bottled up inside. Everyone needed Welsh to be his or her support, and no matter how much he hurt, he would not show the pain. Years later, his daughters would talk about their father and the events of that time. They recalled no sense that their father was absent from them or that he had withdrawn in any way. Never did he fail to stop and play with his girls or say "I love you." Never did the girls go hungry or want for anything. Bill's exceptional character carried the Welsh family through those dark days and set the tone for the remainder of his life.

Welsh could not just neglect his responsibilities while he sorted out his family's life and dealt with his son's death, although the chaos and distraction surrounding Jean's accident and Edna's hospitalization made it difficult to perform his duties. His passion for teaching and coaching diminished, but Welsh followed the advice he had given his players, "Buck up and get back out there." He went back to teaching, and after a time, he realized the importance of the relationship he had with his students, discovering that it helped him to heal. Having a purpose helped him cope, and Welsh found that the best cure for what ailed him was to do what he did best.

Welsh completed the first year in Forest City despite the trauma, and with his help, the teams kept on winning. The 1943–1944 basketball team followed the football team's dominant season in a similar vein, winning won more games than in any season in the school's history. Led by a group of players known as "The Big Four," the team won twenty-four of its twenty-six games and averaged an excellent fifty-eight points per game during the run. It won the North Iowa Conference basketball championship, the Winnebago County basketball championship, and the sectional championship that year. The following year, Welsh's team enjoyed a second undefeated football season, once again winning the North Iowa Conference and Winnebago County championships. During Welsh's first two years, the Forest City Indians did not lose a single conference football game.

Welsh's strength and dedication in the face of his own misfortune inspired his teams and became a motivator when things got tough. With Edna's significant time in the hospital, Welsh developed a routine of driving to Rochester each weekend and whenever else he could get away. She did not recover her strength for over a year and suffered lingering effects of her illness for the remainder of her life. Although Welsh renewed his teaching contract for a second year, he and Edna decided they would cope better by returning to northeastern South Dakota, where the environment for healing would be better in a more familiar area among family.

In basketball, with the graduation of four star players — all of whom went from the basketball court to the war in Europe — the talent cupboard looked a little bare. There remained but one starter, Elton Erdahl, from the legendary team of 1944. However, the youngsters on the team showed great promise, and despite this group's relative youth, Welsh hoped the Forest City Indians might just be the sleeper in the North Iowa Conference during the 1944–1945 season. Despite losing the core of its starting five, the team remained in contention for the conference title until the last game of the season, but it just could not pass a tough team from Belmont; Welsh's boys finished second.

Meanwhile, Welsh had begun to look at alternatives for a new start. The demands of teaching and coaching just did not leave enough hours in the day for him to meet all his obligations; his family needed more from him. As a result, he started thinking about leaving the field of education. As he spread the word among family and friends of his intentions, he learned of a rooming house for sale in Claremont, South Dakota. Not far from Aberdeen and Webster, Claremont was a familiar place with a strong community that was considered a great place to raise children. With Edna's blessing, Bill traveled to Claremont to assess the possibility of turning the rooming house into a game lodge.

The house, a twenty-room "hotel" with four bathrooms, had obviously suffered from deferred maintenance and was in rough shape. Enlarging the rooms and converting the building would offer a diversion and a welcome challenge, Welsh reasoned, but the hotel also represented a less predictable source of income. The pros vastly outweighed the cons in Welsh's opinion, however. Not only could the family work together in the lodge, but they could also live in the quarters beneath the guest rooms. Because it was a seasonal business, Bill hoped he might later have time to teach and coach once he got the lodge up and running. He sensed that it would be therapeutic to be outside, working on the lodge, and more importantly, he would be far away from the memories in Forest City. This radical change would allow Edna time to heal emotionally, and being nearer to extended family and friends would provide the external support they so badly needed.

As an optimist, Welsh looked past the lodge's present condition and determined that there was real potential to create an establishment that could attract moneyed sportsmen to the area, where he could guide them on hunting adventures. On the drive home to Forest City, he concocted a sales pitch with which to convince Edna that they should immediately make an offer on the property. Even so, it was far from easy to leave Forest City. On the day they were to move to Claremont, Bill and Edna traveled to Jean's grave to say their goodbyes. Bill made a silent promise to Brother that he would return someday.

When the Welsh family arrived in Claremont in the summer of 1945, Bill could not help but contrast it to the vast Urbana-Champaign campus and community he had lived in all those years earlier. He had never contemplated life in such a small town. Hardly more than a bump on the prairie, Claremont was smaller than the other communities Bill and Edna had called home. An unremarkable town in the northeastern part of South Dakota with terrain so flat the ditch beside the road represented the largest change in elevation, Claremont was populated by first- and second-generation Scandinavian and German farmers. When the Welshes arrived, the town consisted of approximately two hundred fifty people, two grain elevators, three stores, two milk and egg stations, a bar serving beer with a 3.2 percent alcohol content, two restaurants, a barber shop, a bank, an implement dealer, and three gas stations.

In the spring, the unpaved streets became muddy ruts as the heavy snow melted, and anyone fortunate enough to have a vehicle found driving a real challenge. In the 1930s and early 1940s, those residents who did not farm were likely working for the Civilian Conservation Corps or the Great Northern Railroad.

Following the stock-market crash and up until the outbreak of World War II, times were difficult and money was scarce. Those with imagination found opportunities to make a few dollars doing odd jobs, but it was hard work for little pay. Families did whatever they had to in order to survive. Not until the early-to-mid-1940s did electricity make its way into the Claremont area. The Rural Electrification Administration had been moving power lines into rural areas, but Claremont received electricity later than most. Nights turned truly black, and only kerosene lanterns and candles penetrated the darkness of the plains. Radio linked Claremont with the outside world, and with the war raging overseas, residents tuned in every evening. Neighbors without radios were always welcome to drop by a home lucky enough to have one, where they listened to updates on the progress of the war and big band performances on the *Lucky Strike Hit Parade*.

The residents of Claremont, not far removed from homesteading immigrants, retained many of the basic survival techniques their grandparents had brought with them. Their diet depended upon potatoes, cheese, oatmeal, and whatever vegetables they grew in home gardens or canned from the previous year's harvest. Residents baked their own bread and either raised livestock or purchased meat from local farmers. Because of its costliness, meat was not always a practical choice for the evening meal. Wild game was prevalent, and the residents of Claremont consumed more duck, goose, venison, or pheasant than beef or pork. Milk was available but only as non-pasteurized, non-homogenized raw milk. The residents skimmed cream from this milk for the morning coffee.

Indoor plumbing was available but costly, and many residents collected their water from a well. The artesian water smelled badly and tasted of iron and other minerals, which turned teeth brown if consumed for too many years. Heat, provided by burning corncobs, coal, and any wood that could be found in this area of limited trees, typically came from an iron stove. For those who could afford it, an oil-fired furnace was an alternative. The poorly insulated homes barely held out the cold, and in the midst of a harsh winter storm, frigid drafts often blew throughout the houses. Everyone in town knew what a half moon on a shed meant, and none relished this small and relatively unpleasant hut. It did not help when they were obliged to finish their business with the pages of the Sears, Roebuck, and Company catalog or to stoop to using corncobs or grass if the newest issue was not yet available. Unwittingly, Sears and Roebuck provided the first toilet paper of the prairie with its famous publication. If temperatures were too cold outside or the snow was too deep to make the trip to the outhouse, a makeshift chamber pot solved the problem. Coal for the furnace was a luxury, and many gathered as much as they could from alongside the railroad tracks, where hopper cars transporting coal often shed small amounts to the benefit of industrious residents. Corncobs were more readily available to burn, as they represented a waste product of the farming industry.

Entertainment options in Claremont were extremely limited and most residents relied on their imaginations to escape boredom. During the summer months, baseball dominated

Although this photograph was taken more than fifty years after Welsh lived there, little has changed on Claremont's main street. *Marc Rasmussen Collection*

the town. In winter, children entertained themselves by making snow forts, holding snowball fights, fishing through the ice, riding on sleds, and creating figure eights on the ice-skating rinks. Life would not be easy in Claremont, but the Welsh family knew what they were getting into, and at this point in their lives, the town suited them just fine.

When the family arrived in Claremont, Edna, more realistic than her husband, could not fully envision Bill's plans for the game lodge. She saw only a rundown building with weeds as high as the windows, peeling paint, sagging roof, and an unappealing aroma. Upset by what she saw, she sat down and cried. It was July, and she realized just how much work needed to be done before the hunting season began in October. But they were committed, and if anyone could get the job done, Bill could.

The lodge had shortcomings, but in its favor was its location in the middle of one of the best hunting destinations on Earth. South Dakota held a world-renowned reputation as a sportsman's paradise. In the fall, people from all over the United States arrived to hunt the Chinese ring-neck pheasants that flourished in farmland across the northeastern part of the state. Actors, politicians, sports heroes, and military men all visited, and the chance of a celebrity sighting added to the fun of the opening day of hunting season. The names of hunters who graced the cornfields of the Dakotas included Clark Gable, Ty Cobb, General Jimmy Doolittle, Dwight D. Eisenhower, Ted Williams, Bob Feller, and John Wayne, among others. Pheasants were the main attraction, but the variety of wild game went well beyond those colorful birds.

Claremont was physically located in the middle of the migratory birds' central flyway. Game birds took this route from their nesting grounds in Canada to their winter grounds in the south and central United States. During the migration, over a million birds—mallard ducks, snow and blue geese, and Canadian geese—made their way through the area. The birds found plenty of food in the freshly harvested cornfields, and the numerous lakes and potholes provided a sheltered resting place during their long journey. Resident populations of ducks, Hungarian partridge, and prairie grouse offered variety, as did the increasing whitetail deer population. Improved cover from trees planted to reduce the amount of wind erosion that robbed the area of topsoil during the Dust Bowl years provided habitat for the large animals. The amazing variety of game attracted hunters and visitors from all over the country.

Wishing to tap into these hunting opportunities, Welsh carefully examined the property to determine how to accomplish the conversion into a suitable hunting lodge. He planned to redo the room layout to provide more space for hunters. He

Hall of Fame baseball pitcher Bob Feller (left) starred for the Cleveland Indians from 1936 to 1941 and 1945 to 1956. He was one of the many celebrities to visit South Dakota on hunting trips. *State Archives Collection, South Dakota State Historical Society*

would reduce the number of beds from twenty to twelve and add more amenities. To help with the renovation, Bill's father traveled to Claremont. William Welsh had moved from Aberdeen to California in the late 1920s after he and his wife separated, but now he was needed back in South Dakota. Upon arrival in Claremont, William moved into one of the spare rooms and worked nonstop to help his son renovate the building. He stayed throughout the entire process and made certain that the young family received a little extra attention during this important part of their lives. The men completed the work on the lodge in time for the 1945 hunting season. In just a few months, they replaced what had been an eyesore for the community with a facility in which visiting hunters would feel comfortable.

Edna and her two older girls worked right alongside the men, putting the finishing touches on the lodge with white curtains made from linen bed sheets and blue Naugahyde furniture to spiff up the place. Bill added some masculine touches, focusing on creating an old-fashioned den with cozy chairs, a well-stocked liquor cabinet, a humidor for some fine cigars, and an old slot machine in the corner. Edna, an excellent cook, and her daughters would feed the guests. When it opened, the Welshes' hunting lodge offered clean, comfortable rooms, great food, access to exceptional hunting, a knowledgeable hunting guide, and a place to tell stories, enjoy a cigar or a touch of brandy, and take a chance at fortune on the one-armed bandit. Edna either cooked the wild game harvested during the hunts or Bill's dad cleaned and prepared it for shipping. William used dry ice to cool the game and prevent it from spoiling.

With William Welsh there, both Bill and Edna could take a little time out from their responsibilities to enjoy their girls and each other. Healing was taking place, and the Welsh family gradually grew stronger. Over the next few years, Bill's father never officially moved to Claremont, but he considered it home, and during the football season, he occupied a small house adjacent to the lodge. Edna still struggled with the physical problems caused by her lung damage, but she found the strength to help make the lodge a home for the family. She also brought a breath of fresh air to the residents of Claremont, who welcomed her hospitality, class, and grace. Her time in California and exposure to Hollywood ways and people made her a source of interesting information, and she became a social leader in the community. She inspired the young women of Claremont to move beyond the borders of town and embrace education and travel.

Welsh's Game Lodge garnered success quickly, in part, because of Bill's ability to generate interest in the location. Claremont had never met such a promoter. His life experiences and engaging personality attracted people to him. He projected strength and character, and those who met him immediately trusted him. The lodge was a real departure from the world of coaching, and in many ways, running the lodge represented a vacation from stress, allowing the family to achieve its financial goals. The lodge looked as if it would be an excellent source of long-term income for the family, but in 1947, the South Dakota Legislature issued a ban on nonresident waterfowl hunting, disrupting a strong revenue stream for Bill and Edna. The ban, which would not be repealed until 1970, reduced the potential number of customers for the lodge and would ultimately force the Welshes to convert part of the building into apartments.

Bill Welsh found that the year spent working on the lodge had begun to heal his grief as well as the dilapidated building. As he grew stronger and watched his family integrate into the community, he began to miss the boys he had coached and educated in Kimball, Webster, and Forest City. He came to realize that leaving coaching had not helped ease his pain. He could not help Jean become the man he had envisioned, but he could help others achieve their potential, instead. Salvation for Bill came from the act of helping others, and as time went on, he decided that he could best serve the community by returning to the education profession.

**4** In late 1945, just as the lodge opened for business for the first time, an opportunity came for Welsh to resume teaching. The school at nearby Lake City had lost one of its primary-level teachers and desperately needed someone to fill the vacancy. Despite the early success of the lodge, Bill realized that the family would benefit from the extra income. He accepted the teaching job, but he was not quite ready to take on a coaching position. At the same time, the offer kindled his latent desire to coach. However, Lake City was just too small to field a competitive athletic program, and Welsh began to put out feelers in the Claremont community for opportunities to teach and coach. The high-school basketball team had been struggling for a few years, but the town had achieved some success with its adult baseball teams, having won the 1937 State Amateur Baseball championship, and the community wanted more winners. Knowing that Welsh was interested and aware of the skills he brought, the community called for the school district to hire him. In 1947, with the endorsement of the superintendent and the school board, Welsh became the coach of the Claremont Ramblers, soon to be renamed the Honkers.

In the meantime, the Welsh family continued to grow. The births of daughters Billie Sue and Jeannine Kay followed those of Jane, Judy, and Patty, and Welsh proclaimed that he now had a squad of cheerleaders. At some level, Welsh undoubtedly wanted another son, but he loved his girls and counted his blessings rather than lamented his loss. The commotion in his home always brought a smile to his face. Located a few blocks from Claremont High School, the Welsh lodge was adjacent to a large vacant lot, where many young boys congregated to play baseball, football, or any of a host of games they invented to alleviate boredom. While playing with his daughters, Welsh could hear the sounds of competition across the street, and in time, he found himself interacting with these youngsters, who, he discovered, were eager for more in their lives. Welsh shared with the young men what it was like playing on the same team as the great Red Grange, recounting his stories to the fascinated boys. As Welsh observed them at play, he could not help but notice that they possessed some natural athletic ability, and his keen eye and coaching instincts told him that with a little molding and motivation, Claremont could field a strong football team. Without his intending them to, Welsh's coaching instincts bubbled to the surface. When the opportunity to teach and coach at Claremont High School arrived, he was ready, and the boys were excited at the prospect of him taking over the program.

Soon after the superintendent hired Welsh, the new coach broached the topic of bringing six-man football to Claremont. The six-man game had only recently come into existence, and Welsh relished the possibilities the new game offered to small towns such as Claremont, which could not field an eleven-man team. Encountering no resistance from the community, the school board embraced the opportunity to add the program. In part, the board hoped that adding another sport would, if nothing else, help the players achieve better conditioning for the basketball season. At the start of the 1947 school year, Welsh created the six-man program that would eventually vault him into the National High School Coaches Hall of Fame.

When Welsh introduced the new program, only one of the potential athletes had seen football played, and none of them had participated in a game of competitive football, but they were all enthusiastic about taking part. Welsh had sold the six-man program to the school board with the idea that it would help condition the athletes for other sports. For the young men, conditioning for basketball outside of the season seemed unimportant, as most were farm-hardened, possessed a great work ethic, and did not need special conditioning programs to build up strength. For them, the game appealed for its own sake.

Never having played or coached six-man football, Welsh bought Stephen Epler's book on the sport and studied it long and hard. When he had absorbed all he could about the game, he loaned Epler's book to his players. Each player received instructions to pick a play from the choices presented therein, and Welsh combined the accumulated plays into the first official Claremont Honkers playbook. Given that none of the boys had played or watched football before, the assignment must have been quite a difficult proposition for them and a leap of faith for the coach. That first basic playbook contained only ten plays, and as long as Bill Welsh coached in Claremont and for one year after, the playbook remained largely unchanged. Of course, Welsh tinkered here and there, tweaking the plays where possible; a Welsh team was always exciting despite the limited playbook. Keeping the playbook simple allowed the athletes to become absolute experts on all the plays, and they won games using their flawless execution as well as their athletic ability.

While Welsh set about learning the game and teaching the basics to the players, the school constructed a field upon which they could practice and play. They built seats, goal posts, bathrooms, a scoreboard, and even a concession stand to generate a few dollars of revenue for the program. Welsh recruited volunteers and referees and arranged for all the elements of the spectacle that was six-man football. With the school's limited resources, the proposition was difficult, but Welsh charged into the fray, confident he could get it done.

In recruiting and training referees and volunteers, he could not just pick up the phone and make a call. Because so few people in the area had ever experienced a football game, the coach found that he had to train people in each element of the game. In the process, Welsh became not just the coach but also the ultimate authority on six-man football in the region. He also decided to create a cheerleading squad, teach the girls cheers, and, with the help of Edna and Jane, arrange a means to signal when it was time to start cheering and which particular cheer worked in which situation. For that entire first season in 1947, the cheerleaders looked to the coach for help in every aspect of their program. Bill also worked with the community to carve a football field from the grassland near the school. His own eighty-three-year-old father built the bleachers, refreshment area, bathrooms, scoreboard, and goal posts.

With all the logistics worked out to stage football games, Bill began to build team spirit and improve the overall sports program. The student body, excited about the changes to their sports program, decided to rename their teams, then known as the Claremont Ramblers. They chose the name Honkers in tribute to the large Canadian geese that migrated through the area each year. With the student body behind him and with support from the community, Welsh continued to push for improvements for the entire Claremont's sports program. Claremont High School had been fielding a basketball team for many years

Despite being built before the gym, the American Legion hall in Claremont still stands today. *Marc Rasmussen Collection*

and played in a small gym in the town's Legion Hall. The gym only seated forty to fifty spectators, and the demand for seats vastly exceeded the supply. Welsh worked with the community to gather the resources to build a new gym adjacent to the school, raising money via subscription, arranging for building materials, and coordinating the labor to construct the gym.

Virtually all the residents of Claremont assisted in the project in some form or another, and their accumulated efforts produced an excellent facility for its time and the size of the town. The new gym had capacity for as many as twelve hundred spectators, more than five times the number of people then residing in Claremont. The larger seating capacity meant the high school could attract attendees from outside Claremont and thus generate increased revenues. The school also obtained a facility that became the social hub for the community, adding events such as roller skating. In his first year at the school, Bill effectively transformed a town and its sports programs, which had long been dormant, into one ready to step into the sports spotlight. Through this undertaking, he found a means to pay forward the gifts he had been given in his youth. The spectacular result was the establishment in a tiny town of a sports dynasty that would eventually count two national records to its name.

As a coach, Welsh was a taskmaster and a true professional. Driven, knowledgeable, motivated, and in possession of high expectations for his players, he exhibited a calm demeanor no matter what the situation and commanded respect with his mere physical presence, which was still significant even at the age of forty-four. Because of his personal football talent and exposure to the highest level of achievement in college football, he was a rare resource in such a small community. Like his mentor Bob Zuppke, Welsh insisted on a serious and disciplined approach to the sport, and his teams developed a regimented practice routine. Welsh knew how to energize young men. By allowing the boys to choose the playbook, he had empowered them, and he would often see groups of them working on the various plays on notepads during study hall and talking excitedly about their choices at lunch. His simple action gave the young men a sense of ownership in the program. When the players who started the Claremont streak in 1947 met many years later to talk about the events of those days, each of them recalled the full playbook perfectly.

Welsh devised a simple, but effective method to help his players memorize the plays. An odd number meant the play went left, and an even number meant it went right. Play number One was a handoff to the left of center, while Two went to the right. Three and Four indicated the play went around the ends. Five and Six were passes to the ends with a flip back to the halfback, who was coming in behind the receiver. Plays Seven and Eight were reverses; Nine and Ten signaled double reverses, and they would sometimes throw in a triple reverse just to shake up the other team. The players did not consider the double and triple reverses and the flea flicker as trick plays; they were a normal part of the offense, and in the wide-open six-man game, they were effective plays.

Not satisfied with just ten plays, Welsh occasionally introduced trick plays. The players' favorite started when Welsh would send in a player from the sideline, who waved his hand and shouted, "I'm in for Gus, I'm in for Gus." Hearing this, Gus, or whoever the coach named, would peel out of the huddle and head for the Claremont sideline, being careful to stay behind the line of scrimmage and in the field of play. The trick was that the player coming into the game just kept going to the other side of the field and actually stepped out of bounds. Gus went to the sideline and set up just in front of the coach but did not actually leave the field of play. When the center snapped the ball, Gus ran a streak or post pass route. This play was good for at least one score per game if the other team was not paying attention. A derivative of this play involved sending a player to the sideline to speak to the coach but keeping him in the field of play. The team remained huddled until the last moment, trying to mask the fact that they were one person short, which was a little tough with just six players. When the ball was snapped, the "sleeper" on the sideline followed the same route as the player in the substitution play, but without all the noise and waving of the hand.

The "Long Tom" play was another favorite and involved simple misdirection. The quarterback, receiving the ball from the center, tossed it behind the line to a halfback, who started running to the right. The quarterback immediately reversed field and headed for the opposite sideline. If the defensive players were on task, they would focus on the ball and flow toward it, leaving the quarterback uncovered. Just as the halfback reached the line of scrimmage, he would stop and throw a pass back across the field to the quarterback, who was now an eligible receiver. Another Welsh trick play involved a handoff to the halfback, who put his head down and headed for the line. The end stayed closer to the center, and when the halfback hit the line, he handed the ball to the center or to the end, depending on the play called, while continuing through the line as if he still held the ball. A misdirection of this type confused the opposing team, their coach, and most of their fans. By the time anyone realized what was going on, the ball was across the goal line. Welsh thus had numerous trick plays in addition to the basic ten plays, and while he believed in the highest levels of sportsmanship, he also believed a coach should take advantage of the rules whenever possible.

Bill Welsh's football philosophy based everything on execution of the basics, and he ran his team through drills every practice. The boys participated willingly in this hard work because the coach helped them understand how special a team could be, and they wanted to be that team. He showed them that practice and a positive attitude could trump skill, and he always encouraged them to go into a game expecting a victory. Being a part of the team was a privilege and something to which the boys of Claremont could aspire. Those on the team were part of an exclusive club; a part of something extraordinary. Having made that exclusive club, the boys quickly realized that Welsh's practices would truly prepare them for their games. Among the many things he expected of the young men in his care were quickness and cunning. During practice, he stood on the defensive side of the ball, with the understanding that, if he could see the ball in the course of the offensive play, he would add time to the session. If they wanted to be home by dinner time, his players learned to be sneaky with the ball.

Not only did they need to be quick of thought, they also needed to be strong in body. A physically tough man, Welsh demonstrated the proper techniques of football firsthand, often to the immediate detriment of one of his players. A key member of the inaugural team, Kay Cutler once asked the coach what a stiff arm was and how to use it. Rather than explain the technique, the coach demonstrated it. As Welsh carried the ball toward him, Cutler suddenly felt the lights go dim as Welsh's stiff-arm hit him square in the forehead. With his emphasis on fundamentals, Welsh required proper blocking technique from his players, and the cross-body block became a fearsome weapon of the Honkers' offense. A tackling dummy made from heavy canvas and filled with sand stood surrogate to help players learn to block. They grew to dislike this dummy immensely, but it, along with Welsh's other practice routines, helped them win games.

# TWO

## THE CLAREMONT HONKERS

# THE TALE OF SIX-MAN FOOTBALL

By the early 1930s, football had already reached high levels of popularity at the college level, and high schools clamored to be part of the fun. High schools with an adequate student population and money in the coffers enthusiastically started football programs, and the game quickly grew in scope. In smaller communities throughout the United States, where schools lacked students and monetary resources, fielding a football team often proved difficult, leaving a large number of schools unable to take part in the growing sport. With the advent of the Great Depression and the ensuing economic chaos, the migration from rural communities to areas of greater economic potential impacted school enrollments in small, farming communities throughout South Dakota. For such communities in the decade following the Great Depression, the sport of six-man football arrived at the perfect time. The thousands of games played in the mid-to-late thirties helped distract rural South Dakotans from their economic woes, providing entertainment to those who had little else about which to be excited. Before the development of this version of the game, their only access to football came via distant radio broadcasts or through weekly newspaper coverage, and neither mechanism could capture the thrill of a live game. Six-man football also allowed tens of thousands of athletes from small schools across the country to enjoy a sport otherwise unavailable to them. The game became a national phenomenon, rivaling the eleven-man version for total teams competing at the high-school level.

In rural parts of the United States in the early 1930s, the number of towns with populations of less than five hundred residents exceeded those with more than five hundred by a significant margin. The smallest towns had a difficult time fielding a competitive, traditional football team, as some schools had no more than ten boys available (and some, even less) to play the sport. Even if such schools attempted to field teams, it only took an injury or two to end their seasons. Such a significant obstacle meant that many rural communities decided not to invest in football for their school district. Fortunately, a twenty-five-year-old assistant high-school coach, understanding the importance of sports to small communities, invented the game of six-man football. Stephen Epler was a remarkable individual who, over the course of his career, became famous for more than just his contribution to the game of football.

When he first arrived at Beatrice High School in Chester, Nebraska—his first teaching job—Epler was disappointed at the inability of his school to field a traditional football team. The Little Blue Conference to which Beatrice belonged had never played football simply because a student population of less than thirty boys was inadequate. But Epler loved the game and would not let the small student population in Chester deter him. The school board assured him that if he could come up with a cost-effective scheme to institute the sport, he would have their support. With that preliminary approval, Epler enthusiastically studied the issue, coming across information written by Walter Camp, the venerated and influential Yale graduate widely credited with many important developments in the rules and tactics of football during the 1880s. Camp suggested that a game involving less than eleven players per team was possible. During the 1933 school year, Epler formulated his thoughts and began to develop a down-sized variation of the sport.

Stephen Epler looked more like a librarian than an athlete, with wire-rimmed glasses and an intellectual bearing. His looks deceived, however, as he had grown up playing football and possessed enough skill to play the sport at Cotner Christian College in Lincoln, Nebraska. With the help of the athletic director of nearby Hebron College, William Roselius, Epler worked on the premise of his new game and began to sketch out a rulebook. He wanted to ensure that his new game kept the sport economical so that cost would not be a barrier for small schools. He also strove to make six-man safe in order to give it a wider appeal to parents who had too frequently heard of high-school players being injured or even killed while playing the eleven-man version. But the new game also needed to retain the features of the original sport. High entertainment value, scalability to various numbers of participants, and an open game that was fun to play became his main objectives.

To achieve his objectives, Epler looked long and hard at each position in the eleven-man game, trying to determine the optimal player count. Keeping his goals in mind, he decided that the best opportunity to open up the game would involve eliminating the interior line positions. At the time, the traditional eleven-man game typically employed five men on the offensive line: the center, two guards, and two tackles. The players occupying these positions, due to their size and strength, often caused injuries through double-team blocking and piling-on when tackling. The interior linemen also tended to slow down the game and provided more obstacles for the ball carriers. This tendency, in Epler's opinion, made the eleven-man game lower scoring and less exciting for fans. By eliminating the guards and tackles and forcing the two ends to line up either side of the center, Epler deemed it possible for smaller players to participate and to increase the overall speed of the game. Dropping the interior line positions was a good start, but Epler still had four players in the backfield versus three on the line. He eliminated one of the two halfbacks, leaving a quarterback, a halfback, and a fullback and achieved a nice symmetrical arrangement, which, he reasoned, would meet the goals he had set out for the new sport.

Fewer players and more open space per person also forced Epler to design a playing field with smaller dimensions than the traditional one hundred yards by fifty yards. The six-man field was, instead, eighty yards long and forty yards wide. This change kept the game from becoming simply a speed contest and allowed for actual contact between the offensive and defensive players. Because the game still provided more space per player, Epler decided that first downs would occur only after the ball traveled fifteen yards, as opposed to ten yards in the original game. The teams kicked off from the thirty-yard line to start the game, and the ball was placed on the fifteen-yard line of the receiving team in the event of a touchback. Each contest had four eight-minute quarters. The game allowed players to substitute freely, and they did not have to substitute in and out at the same position. The substitution rules made the game more interesting because players changed positions and, with fewer players available at small schools, diversification rather than specialization was critical in keeping the game going in the event of injuries.

Once Epler had defined his vision for the new sport, he began to refine it. He observed that many injuries occurred at the start of the game or just after halftime, when the player's muscles were tight and their bodies not yet prepared for contact. Epler put rules into place that required a minimum three-minute warm-up just before the start of each half to help prevent injuries. He also knew that many injuries occurred on the extra point try after a touchdown. Rather than settling for a single point by kicking the extra point, more teams would attempt to run or pass it into the end zone for a two-point conversion. A disproportionate number of injuries occurred during these plays, and with the high-scoring game he was developing, it would likely get worse.

To make the kicking option more attractive than the run, Epler changed the dimensions of the goal posts by widening them to twenty-five feet (from twenty-three feet), making them at least twenty feet high, and lowering the cross bar to nine feet to provide a bigger target. He then reduced the points earned for a play from scrimmage after a touchdown to one point and awarded two points for a kick. He also decided to increase the number of points scored for a field goal from the traditional three points to four. The technique for scoring a field goal was to use a drop kick, and since the drop kick came in the normal flow of the offense, it gave the defense one more threat to consider.

Where eleven-man teams required significant protective equipment and at least twenty to thirty players on the team to be successful, the six-man game required only a helmet, a place to play, and as few as eight players on a team. The reduction in players also resulted in exciting games. Where eleven-man teams often relied on sheer power, the six-man game required speed, execution, and deception, all components appealing to spectators. The increased number of pass plays, reverses, misdirection plays, and longer open-field runs kept the spectators entertained. The adapted rules also allowed any player an equal opportunity to score, which appealed to the players who would otherwise have toiled in a guard or tackle position in which their names would be called only if they missed a block or committed a penalty. The six-man "show" offered large scores, wide-open, razzle-dazzle offenses, and spectacular open-field tackles for the benefit of the fans. In a pamphlet promoted on Wheaties cereal boxes, Epler described one of the big arguments for the sport: in the first one hundred games played, six-man football produced twice the number of touchdowns as eleven-man.

A *Time* magazine article entitled "Sport: Six-Man," in October 1937, spelled out the economics of the sport. The cost of equipping a starting squad of six players with a helmet each and a football was less than one hundred dollars. In Nebraska, the cost for a spectator to get into a game was between ten and forty cents. For most teams, the total gate receipts tallied less than fifty dollars, but that amount more than covered the costs.

A visiting team received five dollars for its participation, and the referee took home three dollars for his work.

Once Epler was comfortable with the structure of this new game, he took the Chester school board up on its promise to endorse his plan and received permission to test the game. Knowing he had to prove its viability, he set out to secure teams willing to play the sport. The first-ever game occurred in Hebron, Nebraska, played between two teams recruited from four area high schools. It received high marks from both the players and the fans, and it encouraged Epler to continue developing the game. In 1934, he tested the game's rules and nuances through a series of experimental match-ups. At the end of the year, he published the rulebook for the sport, entitled *How to Play Six-Man Football.*

Epler further refined and clarified his rules as time went on, and each state added its own requirements. For example, all six players, including the center, eventually became eligible to receive a pass. Players on the offensive team could change positions with each play, and players could reenter the game no matter when they left. In South Dakota, as in other states, the players were originally required to wear canvas shoes or softball shoes with rubber spikes to keep both cost and injuries

The Beatrice High School, in Chester, Nebraska, fielded a six-man team around 1934. *Marc Rasmussen Collection*

down. By the mid-1940s, however, metal cleats had become the norm, and officials checked before a game to make certain they were not too sharp.

In 1935, the number of six-man football teams in the country increased to over one hundred fifty. In 1936, this number grew to five hundred, and by 1938, the national association for the game estimated two thousand five hundred teams were participating. By 1940, an estimated five thousand schools across the country played six-man football. With the quick rise in its popularity, All-State and All-American teams were instituted, and Stephen Epler himself chose the first All-American six-man squad and announced the results in December 1939. Such popularity led to considerable newspaper coverage, and in 1941, the *Cumberland Times* in Maryland, for instance, proclaimed: "It is not trick football, exercise football or even football's little brother. It is a fast, heads up, hard-hitting game demanding the utmost of coaches and players and giving the best of fighting competition to the spectators."

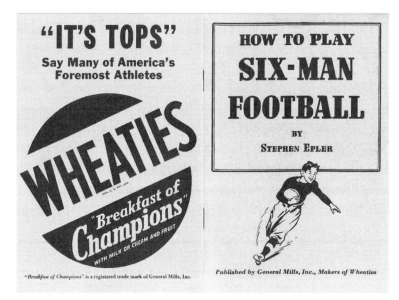

Stephen Epler's *How to Play Six-Man Football* was published by General Mills. *Marc Rasmussen Collection*

**6** When the Claremont Honkers took the field for their first ever six-man football game in 1947, they faced a team from Hecla that had already been playing six-man football for a few years. On 19 September, on their brand new field, the Honkers and Bill Welsh introduced Claremont to this particular brand of football. Neither the Claremont players nor the fans knew exactly what to expect from the contest; although Claremont had played the eleven-man game for a few years in the 1930s, most of the current fans had no idea what this version would be like. The Hecla Rockets, who had already proven to be a real force in the sport, came into Claremont expecting an easy, early-season win. With no way to gauge the abilities of the Honkers, the Rockets were cocky and blind. The Honkers quickly opened their eyes, surmising correctly that the Rockets had underestimated their opponents' abilities.

One player in those early years stood out, and he served notice of his talent in that first game. Affectionately known as "Horse," Donnie Gibbs was a high-school junior with just two years of varsity football to play. But, in those two years, he became one of the most productive football players in the country, amassing points no matter who the opposition. In his 6 foot 3 inch, 190-pound body, Gibbs possessed the greatest individual speed in northern South Dakota. In 1947, he ran the hundred-yard dash in a little over ten seconds, an incredibly quick time for the era and his age. This speed, combined with his large size, allowed Gibbs to devastate his opponents in the wide-open game of six-man football. He destroyed every defense designed to stop him and was especially brutal on those unfortunate enough to attempt to tackle him. Rather than go out of bounds or just go

down when hit, he initiated contact with tacklers, always trying to deliver a bigger blow than he himself received. Former
teammates estimated that he averaged between four and six
touchdowns per game as a Honker. In the eighteen games he
played, the Honkers scored a total of 978 points, averaging 54
per game. If Gibbs averaged five touchdowns, he would have
scored more than half the total points. And he was not just a
football star; he was also an excellent baseball pitcher, basketball player, and runner.

The Hecla players knew Donnie Gibbs from baseball and
basketball, but they did not anticipate what a physical force
he might be in football. In that first game, he quickly showed
them. Hecla won the toss and chose to receive the ball. Claremont kicked off, and Donnie, adrenaline pumping, raced downfield in pursuit of the kick receiver. Having fielded the ball non-
chalantly, the Hecla player looked up to find Gibbs in his face.
The resulting collision caused the fans to gasp as the Honker
hit the kick returner hard, knocking him unconscious and putting him out of the game. One play, one man down. All of a
sudden, the Hecla players knew it was going to be a tough afternoon. The Claremont crew had instantly proved they had
mastered the game. Gibbs, Mickey Vickers, and Bob Stanley
scored touchdowns for Claremont, and the Honkers defense
held the Rockets scoreless well into the second half. By the end

The 1947
Honkers
included
star players
Gibbs, Cain,
and Vickers
(back row).
Hollister
is holding
the ball.
*Welsh Family
Collection*

of the game, Hecla was on the wrong end of a 43 to 6 score. The final tally surprised the Rockets, who were used to running up big scores of their own and holding opponents to low offensive outputs.

The first game was a huge win for Claremont, and it set the tone for future contests, including what already appeared to be a grudge match scheduled at Hecla the following month. Because the towns were just twenty miles apart, the rivalry between Claremont and Hecla sports teams had always been special, and there was something almost primal about this game. The competition between the two teams over the next few years improved both programs, and their quest for excellence

Claremont's all-round star athlete in the early years was Donnie Gibbs, who was featured in an unknown newspaper. *Welsh Family Collection*

inspired other small towns to join the fray. The two schools became role models for small-town football programs in the region, and as Claremont got better, others followed suit, slowly closing the gap in quality. As for Hecla, it would be years before they would find a way to beat the Honkers, but when it happened, it made history.

After the first Hecla game, the Honkers faced a contest with the Leola Pirates, one of the top-rated teams in northeastern South Dakota. At halftime, the Honkers found themselves down by one point and concerned that their winning streak might end after just one game. In the second half, however, Gibbs and his teammates found their legs, and in a third-quarter flurry of activity, the Honkers scored four touchdowns to beat the Pirates by a score of 31 to 22. Upset by the resounding defeat just handed to them, the Leola team demonstrated a lack of sportsmanship, refusing to shake hands after the contest. Given Welsh's strong emphasis on the ethical side of sports, the Leola players' actions did not sit well with the coach and his players.

In the third game of the year, Claremont traveled to Welsh's old stomping ground, Webster, to take on their B team in what would prove to be a rare eleven-man contest. The Honkers only had four reserve players, but that did not deter them, nor did the fact that they had never played eleven-man football. Donnie Gibbs tore through the Webster team for six touchdowns—including one of eighty yards—and passed for another. The score was 32 to 0 by halftime, and the local paper declared that Claremont had unleashed a "super-man" on Webster in the form of Gibbs. The Webster coach exclaimed, "They were just too darn tough for us." The final score was 44 to 7. Welsh took a little extra pleasure from this game as he knew many of the players, coaches, and fans, and he quickly accepted their request for a rematch the following year.

The Honkers took their unbeaten record to Barnard and dispatched the injury-depleted Bears with an efficiency that resulted in the starters spending only five minutes on the field.

In addition to the usual efforts from Donnie Gibbs, including a touchdown on the third play of the game, the Honkers also tallied scores from Red Sanderson, Warren Pierson, Clinton Buffington, Ronnie Odland, Val Cutler, and Kay Cutler. The final score was 45 to 0, but it could have been much worse. The early dominance gave the younger players a chance to test their skills and the fans a chance to see future stars in action. Freshman Harold ("Red") Sanderson, in particular, would go on to have an incredible high-school career.

Like his namesake, Red Grange, Sanderson was a great runner and would earn a Honkers record that Gibbs did not. In 1950, Sanderson's senior year, Red played a little more than half the game against Kidder, but scored eight touchdowns. Since the Honkers often did not kick the points after a touchdown, preferring to run the ball in, Red scored a number of these points as well, and his single-game scoring record ended up at fifty-two points. Red played four years of six-man football at Claremont without ever experiencing a loss. The team's record during that time was 36 and 0, and even though precise records were not kept, he was probably the top scorer in Claremont six-man football history, benefiting from significant playing time in his freshmen and sophomore years due to the large leads generated by the starters.

Having traveled to Leola for their second game, Claremont next hosted the Pirates, in the Honkers' inaugural homecoming event. The game was never really close. Leola had snubbed the Honkers at the end of their first encounter, and they now found themselves up against a spurned opponent. Willie Hollister used "vicious blocking" to turn in what the *Groton Independent* called a "tower of strength" performance, and Gibbs and company ran up a 19–0 lead by halftime. The second string mopped up the demoralized Pirates in the second half. Spurred on by a vociferous crowd, the Honkers sent the Pirates away hurting from a 32–6 loss, their second to Claremont that year.

Now into the second half of the season, the Honkers traveled to Hecla for the rematch of the inaugural game. The Claremont players expected a fevered effort by the Rockets in front of their own crowd. Hecla had a lot to play for; one loss in a season might be a fluke, but a second loss for the Rockets would be a disaster. Unfortunately, the Hecla team had suffered significant injuries to some key players and lacked the ability to slow down the red-hot Honkers offense. Behind touchdowns from Gibbs, Lyle Cutler, Mickey Vickers, Neil Cain, Clinton Buffington, and Willie Hollister, the Honkers pounded the Rockets 57 to 7. One of the stars that day was Mickey Vickers, who chipped in two touchdowns. Equal to Donnie Gibbs in athletic prowess as a baseball player, Mickey was a key figure in Claremont's first eighteen wins as a six-man football team. A dominating runner and defender, Vickers complemented Gibbs's performance with his hardnosed toughness and selfless play. Mickey blocked for Donnie, and a typical Vickers block often led to a Gibbs touchdown. Vickers was also a great baseball player and, along with Gibbs and Neil Cain, went on to play professional baseball for the Watertown Elks team, a farm club for the Chicago White Sox that would win the national championship at that minor league level while the three former Honkers were on the staff.

In the final regular season game of 1947, the Honkers played the Barnard Bears for a second time. In a game stopped at halftime by the mercy rule, the Honkers beat the Bears by a score of 47 to 0. Gibbs scored three touchdowns in the first quarter, with the remaining scores spread evenly among the starters. This win secured the North Central Conference championship for the Honkers and set up an Armistice Day game to be played on 11 November against Montrose, South Dakota. The undefeated Cornbelt Conference champion, Montrose was considered the top team in the southern part of the state. In this first unofficial state championship game for the Honkers, Donnie Gibbs showed his best stuff, scoring three touchdowns in the first quarter alone. Two of his touchdown runs exceeded seventy yards. Montrose put up a tough effort, but it was not enough to defeat the mighty Honkers, and the final score was 40 to 24. Local newspapers estimated the attendance at the game to have topped eight hundred fans, and the proceeds went to the Abbott House orphanage in Mitchell, South Dakota.

The Armistice Day games at Claremont—of which this one was the first—would become a major event in the region over the next several years, akin to a prize fight between two champions; the outcome determined the number one ranking in the state and gave the victor claim to the "Mythical State Championship." The press coined the "mythical" title due to the lack of formal playoffs in the six-man game in South Dakota, and Welsh readily used the phrase, as well. He reasoned that the number-one team should earn a championship. In that first season, the Honkers earned the right to call themselves champions with the win over Montrose. This claim also put Welsh's team on the radar of all the other top teams in the region, and he made it clear that Claremont would take on all comers, never avoiding the chance to compete against the best.

In that inaugural season, the Honkers scored 367 points and held their opponents to just 72. Plaudits for the coach's and the team's success came thick and fast, with the local newspapers calling the undefeated season a "marvelous accomplishment." The squad consisted of fifteen players: Donnie Gibbs, Neil Cain, Willie Hollister, Mickey Vickers, Lyle and Kay and Val Cutler, Clinton Buffington, Bob Stanley, Ronnie Odland, Vernie Swanson, Red Sanderson, Jim Peterson, and Warren and Tim Pierson. Following such a successful first season, Welsh had plenty more boys interested in playing, and he would expand the squad to twenty players in year two of the Honkers run with seven new freshmen.

After the undefeated season, the Claremont boys turned to basketball, and the Honkers had a solid first season under Welsh, finishing as runner up in the North Central Conference to the powerful Andover Gorillas. Moving into the postseason, Welsh took his team to victory in the District IV basketball championship and then lined up against Webster in the Region I opener. Webster defeated the Honkers 53 to 27, and the much larger school went on to win their third state championship in a row. Star Claremont players Donnie Gibbs and Lyle Cutler both made the All-Conference team. Not content with already coaching the football and basketball teams, Welsh also helped Claremont field its first track team in the spring of 1948. A strong believer in continuous conditioning, Welsh reasoned that the boys would benefit physically from taking part in track and field outside of the football season. Given the obvious talent in the school, Welsh expected he would have a decent team, but even he was pleasantly surprised when, behind Gibbs's victories in two hurdles events and third-place finishes in the sprints, they won the Class B Region I track title. Only Gibbs competed at the state track meet, but his incredible talents earned the Claremont Honkers fourth place.

Even before Bill Welsh moved to Claremont, the town had been known for its baseball teams. Baseball in the summertime was an obsession among the boys and men of the town with enough participants to warrant four teams in the State Amateur Baseball tournament. The high-school boys played for the American Legion Junior program. This league pitted their squad against teams from the biggest cities in the state. But despite the disparity, over the course of the season, Claremont defeated teams from Mitchell, Rapid City, Pierre, and Aberdeen on their way to the state championship game against an exceptional team from Sioux Falls. In the playoff rounds, Donnie Gibbs threw his second no-hitter of the year against the Aberdeen Smittys and then followed it up with a third no-hitter against Pierre. Sioux Falls won the championship game, but considering that a team from a town of just over two hundred people was up against one from a city of more than forty-two thousand residents, it was a remarkable achievement.

After such an auspicious first season of football, the majority of the boys returned for 1948, with just Kay Cutler and Clinton Buffington graduating, and Welsh could count on seniors Gibbs and Vickers once again. Despite the incredible success they had achieved the previous year, the Honkers proved to be even more dominant in 1948. By claiming the Mythical State Championship in 1947, Claremont's visibility among its competitors had reached new heights. Each team the Honkers encountered during the 1948 campaign brought the best they had to offer in hopes of defeating the top team in the area. From the beginning of that season until the streak ended years later, every contest took on a championship-game aspect, and the Honkers had to be at the top of their game every week. Coach Welsh received a significant number of requests from schools that wanted to play his team. One of the first challengers he scheduled was the undefeated squad from Selby, which had claimed to be the co-champions in 1947. Welsh appreciated the theatre this game represented and knew it would be popular with the fans. The 1948 schedule also included the top team from Minnesota, Browns Valley, which Welsh challenged to a contest on its home field. Welsh also accepted a challenge from Faith, the best team in western South Dakota, and for the second-annual Armistice Day game, he sought out the Hankinson Pirates from North Dakota, whom many experts touted as one of the best in the country.

Once again, the Claremont Honkers opened the season against the Hecla Rockets, but this time they traveled to Hecla. Still a tough six-man team and stinging from two defeats the previous year, Hecla wanted the opportunity for revenge. Happy to comply, but not content to be the proverbial lamb to the slaughter, Claremont promptly took their opponents right back to 1947 and unleashed a crushing victory. Claremont held Hecla scoreless until late in the fourth quarter while racking up points of their own. Hecla scored a late touchdown to make the final 58 to 6. Five Honkers marched into the end zone, with Mickey Vickers scoring three times, Donnie Gibbs and Lyle Cutler scoring twice, and Pat Vickers and Warren Pierson scoring once each. A freshman in that second season, Pat Vickers, Mickey's younger brother, was considered one of the toughest defenders in Claremont High School's six-man history. At 5 foot 10 inches and 190 pounds, his stocky body proved an immovable object when it came to blocking and tackling. After graduating, Pat went on to play football at North Dakota State University in Fargo. He also excelled on the basketball and baseball teams in Claremont.

Having dispatched Hecla so easily, the Honkers next lined up against the Barnard Bears—a school with a football program that many touted as much improved over the previous year. Unfortunately for the Bears, by the end of the game, the 69–0 score reflected Claremont's superiority. Wilmot followed next and trod a similar path to a 60–0 loss, but in the course of the game, they took out their anger on the Honkers. Neil Cain, the quarterback, was knocked unconscious early in the game, and he sat out with a concussion for the remainder of the contest. Meanwhile, Pat Vickers had two teeth knocked out, but the Wilmot players could not touch Donnie Gibbs, who scored the first two times he touched the ball.

Just as in 1947, Welsh tested his team with an eleven-man

The Claremont Honkers six-man football squad of 1948. *Welsh Family Collection*

contest against Webster B, but this time the game took place in Claremont. Just as in the previous year, Gibbs dominated. He scored five times in Claremont's lopsided 38–0 win. Over the course of the two games against Webster, he was responsible for eleven touchdowns. Webster decided they would avoid the Claremont boys in 1949.

With so few local schools playing six-man football, the schedule pitted teams against each other regularly. Hecla quickly found themselves up against their nemesis once again. And, yet again, the Rockets fell victim to the Honkers. This Claremont victory was a carbon copy of the earlier wins, with their high-powered offense overwhelming an undermanned defense as they ran up a final count of 63 to 6. Donnie Gibbs set the tone for the game, taking the opening kickoff back for a touchdown. Such a comprehensive loss left the hapless Rockets searching for ways to beat this amazing team.

The first feature contest of 1948, Selby versus Claremont, included the two teams claiming ownership of the 1947 state title. Welsh made certain he hyped the game, and his promotional efforts paid off. The two squads, largely unchanged from the previous year, drew a huge crowd to Claremont's field, as the home team proved they were the rightful champions, sending Selby home with a 68–14 whipping. The victory removed any residual doubt over the previous season's conflicting claims to the championship.

Prior to the season, Welsh had anticipated his team's local dominance and had challenged Browns Valley High School in western Minnesota. Browns Valley came into the game on a five-game winning streak of their own, having scored an average of fifty-five points in each victory. In spite of the Minnesota team's reputation as the best six-man team in that state as well as their obvious size and weight advantage, Claremont defeated them 65 to 41, in one of the closer contests of the year.

Having defeated the best northeastern South Dakota six-man

team and the best from Minnesota, the Honkers played their third feature contest in a row in front of a large homecoming crowd in nearby Groton. Claremont was not going up against Groton but was playing Faith in the first game of a two-game schedule that formed part of the festivities. Faith, which was undefeated, had not had an opponent score against them all year. Many observers considered Faith the best defensive team in the state and Claremont the best offensive team, with most experts picking Faith over Claremont. The scoreless streak for Faith's opponents ended just twenty-one seconds into the game when Gibbs took the first handoff and carried it in for a long touchdown. That early strike set the tone for the game, and the Honkers dominated both sides of the ball, winning 77 to 0, dramatically proving the experts wrong.

Bringing home these three marquee victories gave the Honkers bragging rights over two states, but they wanted more. The Armistice Day game would pit the Honkers against the team with the best record in the country at that time, the Pirates of Hankinson, North Dakota. Lest they overlook a team in anticipation, however, Welsh carefully focused his boys on their interim opponent, the Langford Lions, but the Lions provided little resistance to the Honkers' continuing offensive onslaught. Once more, Claremont scored more than sixty points, securing the win 68 to 6. That victory set up the much-anticipated final game of the year against Hankinson. Two thousand spectators "roared their approval" as the Honkers put on a "dazzling performance," securing a half-time lead of 34 to 0. In the second half, the heralded Hankinson defense finally worked out Claremont's schemes and limited the Honkers to just one more score, but try as they might, the Pirates could not find the end zone themselves. As is so often the case, the contest had not lived up to expectations, and Claremont defeated what Welsh called the best team that they had faced that season by a final score of 45 to 0.

The Honkers recorded ten wins and no losses for the 1948 season, and with victories over the best six-man teams in both Minnesota and North Dakota, they took the mantle of the mythical three-state football champions. In the process, Claremont set the national scoring record for six-man teams with an amazing 608 points and, once again, ended the year ranked number one in South Dakota. The 1948 Honkers team consisted of Neil Cain, Lyle and Val Cutler, Mickey and Pat Vickers, Willie Hollister, Donnie and Lincoln Gibbs, Bob Stanley, Warren and Tim Pierson, Ronnie Odland, Vernie Swanson, Harold ("Red") Sanderson, Jim Parkin, Gerald Henley, Jim Peterson, Paul Feser, Bruce Traphagen, and Dalton Perkins. After two seasons of playing football, Welsh had coached his teams to eighteen wins. Not content with victories on the football field, four of the six starters—Neil Cain, president; Donnie Gibbs, secretary; Lyle Cutler, treasurer; and Mickey Vickers, student council—were also elected as class officers by their peers.

The boys' success continued onto the basketball court, as many of the same players came close to carrying the Honkers into the State B basketball tournament for the first time in their history. Along the way, the Honkers defeated the Andover Gorillas on their home court—the first time any team had done that in seven years. The famous victory happened despite the fact that Donnie Gibbs fouled out in the third quarter, quickly followed by Mickey Vickers and then Lyle Cutler. The basketball team went undefeated in the regular season, breezed through the District IV tournament and into the Region I tournament, where they eventually lost to Sisseton. Along the way, they defeated Groton and, in the regional tournament consolation round, Webster, the defending state champions. The Honkers earned the newly formed Lake Region Conference (LRC) championship during both the regular season and the conference tournament. The basketball team ended their amazing season with twenty-five wins and one loss. Donnie Gibbs was elected to the All-Conference team, as was Lyle Cutler.

In the spring of 1949, Gibbs once again proved his athletic talent, repeating his track-and-field performance in the Regional I meet by winning all four events he entered. This time, though, Gibbs had a Honker teammate at the state tournament. Willie Hollister won the regional title in both the shot put and the discus, earning his place alongside Donnie. At the state meet, the duo combined to win the title for Claremont. Gibbs scored enough points individually to win the meet, but second-place finishes in both throwing events by Hollister bolstered the overall point total. Gibbs won both hurdle events and took second in both the sprints. He also set a new state record for the high hurdles in the finals.

Welsh stands next to his star runner, Donnie Gibbs, prior to the 1949 track season. *Welsh Family Collection*

# THE STREAK CONTINUES, 1949-1953

As the Claremont boys turned their thoughts from baseball to football in the fall of 1949, they realized that two of their biggest stars, Donnie Gibbs and Mickey Vickers, would not be joining them on the field. Both had graduated in May, and Welsh now turned to a younger group, many of whom had played significant roles on the team in 1948. Although the fearsome running duo was no longer available, Welsh still had a tough team, winning nine more in a row in 1949 as the domination continued. The faces in Welsh's squad were young, but they already had a lot of experience in winning football games, having spelled the previous year's starters early in the games. The next generation of stars included Red Sanderson, Frank Pierson, Pat Vickers, Lincoln Gibbs, Val Cutler, and Bruce Traphagen. Joining them in practice and on the field were Vernie Swanson, Paul Feser, Sam and Gary Pulfrey, Dalton Perkins, Jim Parkin, Gary Odland, Jack Kolbo, Jim Peterson, Ronnie Odland, and Tim Pierson. Smaller and less skilled than some of their predecessors, this group made up for their physical shortcomings with sheer determination.

The key offensive players in 1949 were Pat Vickers and Red Sanderson. These young men would go on to become two of the most productive players in Honkers history. Another star from the core group was Frank Pierson, a shifty quarterback, who was a threat as a passer, a runner, and a kicker—the classic six-man triple threat. He contributed equally well in basketball and was considered one of the top athletes for the Honkers. His most impressive accomplishments on the football field came in 1952, his senior year, when he started at quarterback and was named to the All-State first team.

Welsh feared that the drop in talent might put an end to the impressive streak, but their immense determination to win overcame the deficit, and the young team opened the season with a win over Barnard 46 to 7, impressing reporters and the coach alike. They may have lost Gibbs and Vickers, but Claremont did not lose that game. Nor the next, as it turned out. Against Wilmot, in the second game of the year, the whole Honkers team had a chance to participate in the game, and seven players scored at least one touchdown. The Honkers scored in excess of seventy points for the first time that season, while holding Wilmot to just thirteen. The Claremont boys followed with lopsided wins against both Kidder (62 to 32) and Bristol (58 to 11) before facing a powerful, undefeated Pierpont team that nearly knocked them off their pedestal at the top of South Dakota's six-man football scene. For the first time, the Honkers faced a real challenge in a game, as Pierpont, a slightly larger town than Claremont, had the Honkers down 20 to 8 at halftime. Welsh fired up his charges in the locker room with one of his famous pep talks, and the Honkers mounted a fero-

With Gibbs, Cain, and Vickers gone, the 1949 Honkers had a much more youthful look to them as they prepared for the season. *Welsh Family Collection*

cious rally in the third quarter, while exhibiting solid defense to finish the game with a 28–20 win.

Pierpont had at least demonstrated that it was possible to score on the mighty Honkers, but in 1949, high-school teams in South Dakota did not use film to scout opponents, and the magic formula remained a Pierpont secret. As Selby prepared to face their tormentors once more, they must have longed for such knowledge. Claremont traveled to Selby for the second game in that rivalry, playing in front of an excited homecoming crowd for the second game in a row. Just a week later, Claremont played in front the largest crowd in Honkers' history when Browns Valley came to Claremont. The Honkers, feeding off the energy of those large audiences, won both games, scoring a total of ninety-nine points and allowing just nineteen between the two opponents. Clearly, the raucous environments did not faze the young Honkers.

In the first of these two games, Claremont held Selby scoreless while piling in thirty-nine points of their own. Red Sanderson scored with the most dramatic play of the game. Fielding a punt at the ten-yard line, Red charged towards the oncoming Selby players and used his skill to find a gap. He raced through the hole, and seventy yards later, he crossed the goal line. Unfortunately, one of his teammates had committed a foul, negating the play. Not to be deterred, Sanderson took the next handoff and, almost without being touched, rushed another seventy-five yards into the end zone. The referee could find no fault this time, and the touchdown counted. Despite outweighing Claremont by twenty pounds per boy, Browns Valley also fell to the Honkers. Welsh's tactics utilized speed and trick plays to overcome such physical hindrances, and the Honkers hammered Browns Valley 60 to 19. As usual, Sanderson was heavily involved in the scoring, passing for four scores alone. This victory notched up twenty-five consecutive wins for the mighty Honkers. Next, Claremont thrashed Langford by a score of 77 to 14, to set up the Armistice Day contest against the Hecla Rockets.

As the big game approached, the two-day festivities that encompassed the third-annual Armistice Day game began to take shape. For Ronnie Odland, not only did he have to prepare for the game, he also had to prep for his potential coronation as the king of the carnival. Those preparations did not affect his performance though, and in an extremely competitive game in front of a crowd of more than one thousand people, the Honkers defeated the unbeaten 1949 Hecla team by a score of 31 to 19. The Claremont faithful endured some moments of tension in the game, however, as their boys gave up touchdown runs of thirty and seventy-five yards as Hecla's players strove for a way to beat Claremont. The game culminated another great season as the wins—now standing at twenty-seven without loss—just kept coming for the Honkers. At the end of the season, Pat Vickers, Red Sanderson, and Val Cutler were elected to the Lake Region Conference All-Star team. After the 1949 season, the Honkers had scored a total of 1,447 points during the three-season run, for an average offensive output of 54 points per game. For the third year in a row, they ended the season as the number-one team in the state.

Once again, Welsh put his football coaching to one side and concentrated on basketball and track, but as the 1950 football season approached he grew ever more excited about the potential for his Honkers to outdo even their own illustrious predecessors. The 1950 team proved him right and continued to dominate the competition, with the Honkers maintaining their position as the best of the best in the Dakotas. In many ways, this group had the most successful year in the history of Claremont six-man football. The players had now started for a year, and they brimmed with confidence. That confidence, however, was shaken in the first quarter of the first game of the season when the team played sloppily against the perennially-weak

Barnard Bears. In a steady downpour, Claremont fumbled a number of times before they got their act together. Fortunately, the Honkers overmatched the light and inexperienced Bears, and Claremont prevailed 46 to 0, with Pat Vickers scoring four touchdowns. In the starting lineup for the first time, Lincoln Gibbs added two of his own.

Practice must have gone well following the Barnard game because, in game number two, Claremont controlled the play from the beginning, and in front of a standing-room-only crowd, the Honkers crushed the Langford Lions 87 to 6. Bruce Traphagen and Lincoln Gibbs each scored three touchdowns in the game. Kidder came next, but they could not halt Claremont either and were soundly defeated by a score of 50 to 0. Vickers, Gibbs, Jim Peterson, Paul Feser, and Traphagen did the damage with long scoring runs against an injury-handicapped Kidder team for their thirtieth win. The juggernaut continued. Claremont beat up on the Bristol Pirates by a score of 80 to 13. Vickers and Glen Holznagel each scored three touchdowns with long runs against a weak defense. Four other players joined in the scoring fun as the Honkers appeared unstoppable.

The 1950
Honkers.
*Welsh Family
Collection*

Welsh had, once again, scheduled a tough challenge game, and this season Claremont took on Plankinton, whose Warriors enjoyed an eighteen-game winning streak, having won thirty-three of their past thirty-four games. In order to attract opposition of such quality, Welsh had agreed to pay an appearance fee of $375 to Plankinton to offset the cost of traveling the one hundred sixty miles from just west of Mitchell. Plankinton lived up to its billing as one of the "state's leading football exponents," giving Claremont a torrid time. However, with unusually physical play, Claremont led 14 to 8 at halftime on the back of scores from Peterson and Sanderson. In the third quarter, the momentum shifted. Plankinton had driven all the way to the one yard line, but for four consecutive downs, the Honkers defense held firm and denied the touchdown. Soon afterwards, the Honkers reached Plankinton's five yard line, and Vickers rushed in to give Claremont some breathing room. In the fourth quarter, Vickers intercepted a pass and ran it twenty yards for a touchdown to seal the game and make the final score 28 to 8.

The following week, against the Pierpont High School team that had nearly defeated Claremont the previous season, the

This 16mm frame from the 1950 game against the Hecla Rockets shows the relatively unusual sight of the Honkers punting the ball away. *Marvin Rasmussen Collection*

Honkers took the mystery out of the outcome early and beat their rivals 72 to 10. Pierpont had only lost one game that year, and the contest was once again expected to be close. Claremont took no notice of the expectations, and every Honker scored at least one touchdown. Sanderson scored three times in the rout, while Pierson and Vickers each secured two.

Not content with one challenge game, Welsh also contacted Linton, North Dakota, losers of but one game in five years and generally regarded as the best team in North Dakota in 1950. The population of Linton was more than sixteen hundred at the time, more than six times that of Claremont, but despite that advantage and their own success, Linton came into Claremont expecting a close game. Even so, Linton was unprepared for the powerhouse they faced, and they succumbed to Claremont's offensive execution as well. The Honkers left Linton in the dust, scoring a 72–0 victory. Gibbs, Pierson, and Traphagen all dashed for touchdowns of more than fifty yards, while Sanderson provided the highlight of the game. His seventy-five-yard touchdown run was the longest of the game and provided evidence of both his own skill and the offensive scheme put in place by Welsh. Also showcasing Welsh's training was Bruce

Claremont's defensive team did not often spend much time on the field in the 1950 season, but in this frame, Hecla's halfback tries to evade the Honkers' pursuit. *Marvin Rasmussen Collection*

Traphagen, an exceptional athlete who had come into his own that season. He earned Lake Region Conference honors in both football and basketball, and he offered Welsh leadership and yet another scoring option in both sports.

Having demolished the strong Linton team, the Honkers then faced Java at home. Looking to test their six-man team against the best in the state, Java discovered that they were not yet ready for that level of competition. On the long ride back to Java, they had time to ponder the 78–19 beating that came at the hands of Welsh's charges. The victory against Java set up yet another big Armistice Day game against Claremont's archrival Hecla Rockets. Hecla was again undefeated for the year, and the team considered it their turn to take over as the best in the state. Playing on Hecla's home field in front of a huge crowd, expectations ran high.

Armistice Day fell on a Saturday, and for once, the weather was good for this big game. The winner would be the Lake Region Conference champion, undefeated for the season, and hold the mythical state champion title for 1950, as well. Despite the high expectations, the Rockets were not yet ready to defeat the defending champions. The game started poorly for them

In another 16mm frame, Claremont defenders try to bring down a Hecla runner. *Marvin Rasmussen Collection*

when Claremont's linemen broke through Hecla's offensive line and tackled the halfback in the end zone for a safety. On the ensuing kickoff, Red Sanderson stood ready to receive the ball. Hecla could not stop Red, and he knew it. Catching the ball from the kick, Sanderson shifted quickly into top gear and ran it back for a touchdown. Three more touchdowns made the score 29 to 0 at the end of the first quarter. The biggest scare of the season for the Honkers came in the second quarter when Pat Vickers, who had been involved in most of the scoring to that point, went down with an injury. The Claremont faithful hushed, but he shrugged off the painful ankle and carried on. Fortunately, with Claremont so dominant, the second team played the remainder of the game. Even though Hecla managed to equal their points total from 1949, they were no match for the Honkers, and the final score was 73 to 19.

The undefeated 1950 Honkers were Pat Vickers, Red Sanderson, Tim and Frank Pierson, Jim Peterson, Lincoln Gibbs, Paul Feser, Sam, Gary and Rex Pulfrey, Bruce Traphagen, Glen Holznagel, Gus and Dalton Perkins, Jim Parkin, Jack Kolbo, and Gary Odland. Peterson, Sanderson, Vickers, and Tim Pierson all made the All-Conference team. To this point, the Claremont winning streak stood at thirty-six games.

Ten months later, the 1951 season started where the previous season left off, with another rout. The Waubay Dragons were the opponent this time, and from the opening kick, the outcome was never in doubt. Claremont led 44 to 0 at halftime as Pat Vickers, Bruce Traphagen, and Lincoln Gibbs all found the end zone with regularity. Even with the second string taking over, the final was 70 to 0. Waubay had not tested the Honkers significantly, however, and Welsh was unsure how his latest group of players would perform against their first feature opponent of the year.

Scheduled to play Plankinton on Plankinton's home field, the Honkers knew they would have a tough game. Plankinton had been strong opponents the previous couple of years, and although Welsh had warned his charges against complacency, Plankinton's initial onslaught led to an early lead, shocking the Honkers into action. The Honkers tied the game back up, but Plankinton quickly scored again. For the first time in a long time, Welsh's boys found themselves with a real game on their hands; for the first time in two years, an opposition held a lead against Claremont. The shock, however, did not last much longer. Claremont scored in the second quarter and added an extra point to take a halftime lead of 13 to 12. In the second half, the old Claremont style came to the fore once more, and Pat Vickers scored four touchdowns to give the Claremont squad a 39–24 victory.

Following the Plankinton road trip, the Honkers took on a team from nearby Frederick, who, while new to six-man football, wanted to test itself against the best. They soon discovered that Claremont was not a good team to train against. Coach Welsh put everyone on the Honkers team into the game, with the second string getting most of the playing time, but even with Welsh rotating his players, Claremont won the game 94 to 49. The game was memorable for the highest score the Honkers achieved in their record-setting six-man football run.

The next two games were easy victories as well, as Claremont dispatched Columbia 53 to 20 and Bristol 64 to 24. Bruce Traphagen and Lincoln Gibbs provided the big offensive sparks for the Honkers with typically strong runs and dominating play. After five games, Claremont stood atop the conference standings and had dispatched their opponents in comprehensive fashion. Since Bill Welsh had formed Claremont's six-man football team, it had won forty-one games on the trot. If they could win the next contest, they would tie the national record for consecutive wins.

Fittingly, the forty-second game came against an also undefeated team from Pierpont. Over the previous four years, Claremont's fan base had grown massively. As a result, a huge crowd from all over the area traveled to Pierpont to witness this historical contest. Having been thrashed so comprehensively the year before, Pierpont was determined not to be the victim once again, but in a bloody, tough gridiron contest, Claremont claimed national bragging rights as they vanquished Pierpont 56 to 26. Up until Welsh's Honkers grabbed this win, a team from Bryon, Wyoming, had held the longest unbeaten streak. The local media noted with glee that a South Dakota school had joined Bryon, but Welsh already had his mind on the upcoming game with Langford and the chance to hold the record all to themselves.

On 25 October, Claremont stood ready to claim the record for consecutive wins as its own. Gus Perkins rushed for three touchdowns, and Pat Vickers played a great defensive ballgame as Claremont came away with a 57–7 victory in front of Langford's large homecoming crowd that included Bill's father. Having seen his son's team set the national record, William Welsh headed back to California not needing to see the final game of the season. As the players celebrated, Claremont's followers cheered their coach and his amazing accomplishments. This milestone captured the attention of the *Aberdeen American*

The 1951 Honkers team featured four All-Conference squad members. *Welsh Family Collection*

*News*, which ran a long article on the feat, including Welsh's photograph. Forty-three consecutive wins and counting, the best among all six thousand six-man teams in the nation, the Honkers legend continued to grow.

Claremont once again finished the season against the tough squad from Hecla. Despite the fact that this annual game had developed into a fierce rivalry, the Honkers still had too much skill and determination for the Rockets. Behind the usual dynamic play of Vickers, Gibbs, and Traphagen, Claremont prevailed by a score of 50 to 14. For the fifth consecutive year, they defeated all competition, and there was no end to the streak in sight. Claremont ended the season as the Lake Region Conference champions and the top-ranked team in the state once again. Lincoln Gibbs, Gus Perkins, Pat Vickers, and Bruce Traphagen all made the All-Conference team.

At the culmination of the season, Claremont's devoted followers had a banquet to honor the national-record setters. Gov-

Having surpassed the previous national record, the Honkers celebrated their ongoing streak at a banquet following the 1951 season.
*Welsh Family Collection*

ernor Sigurd Anderson, a big football fan, spoke at the event about a coach's responsibility to create character amongst his charges and condemned the programs that produced "athletic bums" who fixed games to profit from gambling. Mylo Jackson, the athletic director of Aberdeen Central High School, also attended and spoke about the duties and responsibilities of being a coach. Coach Welsh introduced all the players who had participated in the five-year streak, and in thanks for his efforts, the players presented him with a wristwatch. The popularity of the Claremont team created some logistical problems for the Welsh family. So many folks attended the banquet that Bill and Edna were left without babysitters for their daughters, and they were forced to drive to nearby Amherst to drop the girls off with a family friend. Everyone in Claremont was at the soiree.

A few weeks after the dinner, the Aberdeen Athletic Boosters invited Welsh to speak at their party. At the event, he confessed that he thought the streak would end with this particular group of players. He had doubts about the team's chances in 1952 because only a few starters from the 1951 squad would return, and the resulting team would be smaller in stature than previous teams. Welsh revealed one of his coaching secrets, telling the assembled group that he did not believe in scrimmaging at practice. With a six-man club, he worried that the boys might leave their best play on the practice field, diminishing their game performance and increasing the potential for injury. The Honkers only scrimmaged early in the season until the players mastered their positions. Welsh also discussed his practice of inviting the toughest competition available to play Claremont on its home field. Some of those teams, especially those from North Dakota and Minnesota, traveled great distances in order to play the Honkers, and Claremont had to pay some of the top teams a guarantee of as much as three hundred dollars to play. Due to the widespread interest generated as a result of such high-level clashes, Claremont made significant money for their athletic program at these events despite the large advance.

Following the football season, the basketball team took over. With football stars Gibbs, Vickers, and Traphagen leading the way, the team recorded twenty-one wins and three losses, and the Honkers ended the year rated third in the state. The three stars earned All-Conference honors, and the Honkers basketball team won the New Year's Day trophy, the regular season Lake Region Conference championship, and the conference tournament. Changes to the district tournament alignment meant that Claremont now had to face the highly skilled Britton Braves, and the Honkers duly lost to the Braves in the finals. Despite the loss, the team had done so well that year that members of the community decided to fund a trip for the team to the state basketball tournament in Sioux Falls as a reward.

As the basketball season ended, Welsh's attention turned once more to the track team. In the spring of 1952, he attended a meet in Mitchell and afterwards met a group of coaches at a restaurant to discuss the upcoming state meet. As he was driving back to his hotel in the dark, he encountered another car cresting a hill with its lights on bright. Due to his eye injury in college, Welsh struggled with night vision, and the oncoming lights temporarily blinded him. His car slipped off the concrete to the right, caught some soft ground, and went down the ditch, rolling end over end eight times. Ejected from his car, Welsh lay broken and bleeding in the ditch for a number of hours before medical help arrived. He suffered a head injury and multiple broken bones, and the required recovery time kept him off work until the fall. The head injury was significant enough to cause him pain for the remainder of his life and affected him significantly during periods of stress. Fortunately, despite the severity of the accident, Welsh recovered and was able to resume his duties in time for the 1952 football season.

When Welsh slid off the road that fateful night, Lincoln Gibbs, Pat Vickers, and Bruce Traphagen, the stars of his 1951 squad, had all been in the last stages of their high-school careers. With the graduation of those players, Welsh now had a lot of work to do in order to retool the team. However, because of the Honkers' large margins of victory in past years, those players who would inherit the responsibility as starters had already experienced significant playing time and were well prepared for the challenge. Their first game had some awkward moments when Claremont lost multiple fumbles to Waubay early on, but the Honkers recovered quickly, and three touchdowns each for Bill James and Gus Perkins led to a 37–6 victory and eased Welsh's recovery even further.

Against Langford in the second game of the season, Claremont eliminated the technical errors from the first game. Welsh had spent more time than usual in practices that week working on the handoff between the center and the quarterback, as well as on proper ball-carrying techniques. The hard work paid off in a 47–7 victory over Langford. For the second game in a row, Bill James scored three touchdowns. Gary Pulfrey scored two of his own in a balanced performance for the team. Having been overshadowed in 1951 by the illustrious trio of seniors, James was quickly making a name for himself.

Against Veblen the following week, Claremont faced the toughest competition they had encountered in years. The Veblen squad boasted a multi-year undefeated streak and was determined to defeat the champions. Like Welsh, the Veblen coach, Harold Gab, had never coached a losing six-man football game, and he brought an excellent team to this contest. Despite being a mere fifty-five miles apart, the two schools played in different conferences and had never played each other before, but the unfamiliarity did not help Veblen. The Honkers won the game 13 to 6, aided by a great defensive performance. For the first time in Honkers' history, an opposition had held them under twenty points. Veblen's effort also resulted in the closest margin of victory the Honkers had ever experienced. The two touchdowns scored by Bill James were just enough to pull this one out of the fire, while the defensive play of Gus Perkins and Frank Pierson played a large part in the win.

Even though the Honkers were winning, Welsh's concerns about the transition from the previous squad to this one seemed justified in the next couple of games. Against Columbia's experienced squad, the Honkers faced another tough game. Columbia was loaded with talented players, and Claremont had to score two touchdowns in the fourth quarter to eke out the win. Behind at halftime by a score of 8 to 7, Claremont relied on Gus Perkins in the second half. He scored all four touchdowns for the Honkers, including a seventy-five-yard kickoff return to start the second half, which immediately changed the momentum and set them on the way to another win. Claremont next faced coach Lawrence Blood's Bristol Pirates, another tough team that had not lost a game in 1952. For the third game running, Claremont's opponents gave them all they could handle, but the Honkers pulled off the win by a score of 38 to 31. Parity was finally coming to the Lake Region Conference, bringing more of a challenge to Claremont's domination.

Finally, seeking their fiftieth win in a row, the Honkers came to the next game ready to play. The game plan was so well executed against a talented Pierpont squad that Welsh proclaimed

1952

A relaxed group of Honkers prepares to defend its streak at the start of the 1952 season. *Welsh Family Collection*

it the game of the year. The final score was 50 to 20. A match with Frederick, a much-improved team since the previous year, followed. The Honkers played a balanced game with a number of players scoring touchdowns. Frank Pierson did the most damage as he ran for four touchdowns against the Vikings. Marvin Rasmussen, getting some of his first extended game experience, and Gus Perkins were instrumental with their stout defense and offensive output.

Isabel came east from the Cheyenne River Indian Reservation to Claremont to try its luck against the champions but returned home as victim number fifty-two. With an imposing 185-pound running back named Heck, Isabel had a real offensive weapon, but even that was not enough. Winning the toss, Isabel chose to receive the ball first. They took control of the opening drive, using Heck extensively to march down the field and score quickly for an 8–0 lead. Claremont fought back, and at the end of the second quarter, they had scored twice to lead 13 to 8. In the second half, the Honkers gained control of the game, turning up the heat and clicking on the offensive side of the ball. They gave up another touchdown, but scored three more of their own to seal the win 31 to 14. The stars of the game were Marv Rasmussen, Gus Perkins, and Frank Pierson, who had finally taken up the mantle of the 1951 triumvirate of Gibbs, Vickers, and Traphagen.

In the final contest of the year, Claremont took on the Hecla Rockets in the Armistice Day game. The rivalry was as strong as ever, and with singular focus, Hecla continued to improve their program with the goal of beating the Honkers. Both communities looked forward with great anticipation to this game each year, but in 1952, the Claremont fans had more cause for worry than usual. In comparison to previous teams, this year's Honkers had not won many games in convincing fashion. But the Honkers faithful need not have worried. With exceptional play by Rasmussen, Gary Pulfrey, Bill James, and Frank Pierson and the scoring of Gus Perkins, Hecla went home frustrated, again. This time it was a 49–12 beating.

Clearly, the 1952 team was showing the strain of carrying a winning streak that had lasted six full seasons. They survived a number of narrow escapes and saw the overall quality of opponents improve. The boys demonstrated great character to continue the streak, but it was the heyday of six-man football in South Dakota, and challengers had multiplied. The number of schools playing the game had increased to 110, and in a survey conducted by students at South Dakota State University, the average number of players on six-man football squads throughout the state was just over twenty. At the same time, there were seventy-four eleven-man teams in South Dakota with an average of almost forty-seven players per team. Overall, nearly five thousand athletes competed in football in South Dakota during the 1952 school year. In some ways, this year was probably Welsh's best as a six-man football coach. His squad did not include talent comparable to the previous years, and the quality of the opposition had improved. Leading Claremont to another undefeated season emphasized Welsh's ability.

Frank Pierson, Marv Rasmussen, Gus and Owen Perkins, Roger Andrews, Donnie Knecht, Rex and Gary Pulfrey, Bill James, Donnie Swanson, Jack Kolbo, Chuck Anderson, Arlen Warwick, Percy ("Junior") Benedict, and Gary Odland had formed the 1952 version of the all-conquering Claremont Honkers. Claremont once again earned the Lake Region Conference championship and mythical state champions status. No team other than Claremont had won the conference championship in the short history of the Lake Region Conference. All-Conference players for 1952 were Gus Perkins, Marv Rasmussen, Frank Pierson, and Gary Pulfrey. In Welsh's estimation, this team was not as physically tough as past teams, but they had shown a real determination to come from behind to win games. At the end of the 1952 season, the Honkers' winning streak stretched to fifty-three consecutive games, and their legend continued to grow.

Many of the boys now switched from helmets to hoops as the basketball season quickly clicked into gear. The basketball squad for the 1952–1953 school year was strong, with Marv Rasmussen and Gus Perkins stepping up to carry the offensive scoring load. Rasmussen led the team, sinking just over nineteen points a game, and in a year expected to be down for the Honkers, they won twenty-one games and lost five. They repeated as the LRC champions and once again faced the Britton Braves in the District III tournament. Unfortunately, Welsh had not yet figured out a way to beat the Braves, and his squad lost to them again, ending their season. The young basketball team gained some great experience and continued to prove that Claremont was much more than just a football school.

In 1953, the seventh year of the Claremont Honkers six-man football winning streak, the schedule included a group of teams that had had years to consider Welsh's offense and determine ways to counter it. Welsh put together a tough ten-game schedule with teams that Claremont had played at least once during its streak, mostly Lake Region Conference opponents. First up, the Honkers, in front of their home crowd, dispatched Andover 53 to 21. The Perkins brothers, Gus and Owen, as well as Marv Rasmussen, made long runs for touchdowns. Gus had established himself as a lynchpin in Welsh's high-powered offense the previous season, and now it looked as though his younger brother would join in the fun. Waubay followed the next Friday, and in the largest margin of victory for the 1953 season, Claremont beat the Dragons 60 to 19. The game started badly for Waubay as Marv Rasmussen scored on the first play from scrimmage, ripping the ball from the Dragons' halfback and carrying it in for a touchdown. Gus Perkins, at his best once again, contributed long touchdown runs, including a seventy-yarder.

A week later, in a game that had the Claremont fans worried,

Veblen nearly pulled off the upset of the year. Veblen's team had continued to evolve and gain confidence, and with excellent coaching, they were a team to be watched. The Veblen boys stymied Claremont's vaunted offense, and it took a late score and one-point conversion for Claremont to win the game; the final score was just 13 to 12—Claremont's narrowest margin of victory during the streak. Columbia proved less competitive than Veblen, even though they had not lost in the current season and only suffered defeat once (to Claremont) the previous year. Claremont used the game to catch their breath after the scare the previous week. The Comets fell to Claremont 38 to 13, giving the "Honks" their fifty-seventh consecutive win. The score was 20 to 0 after the first quarter, allowing Welsh to play his reserves most of the second quarter. The Perkins boys once again led the way, while Marv Rasmussen and Junior Benedict also had great games. The Bristol Pirates followed Columbia. Playing in a horrible downpour and miserable field conditions, the Claremont boys won the game going away, 46 to 13. Gus Perkins had two seventy-five-yard touchdown runs, continuing to make a strong case for All-State honors at the end of the season.

No one seemed able to halt Claremont's success. The next opponent, Pierpont, had done nothing in the previous three years to indicate that the team might challenge the Honkers. However, the Pierpont players fought hard against the team in green and threw every weapon they had at Claremont. Trick plays flowed out of both coaches' playbooks. At the end of the contest on Pierpont's home field, Claremont limped away with the win, relieved to have survived their opponent's onslaught. The final score was 38 to 28, with Gus Perkins scoring all five of Claremont's touchdowns.

During this hard-fought game, a controversial event tested the sportsmanship that Welsh had worked so hard to instill in his players. One of Pierpont's key players was involved in some questionable conduct early in the contest. After a second flagrant incident, the referees tossed him out of the game. The young man remained on the sidelines, pacing back and forth as his teammates struggled against their rivals. As the third quarter began, however, the Claremont players noticed a new player had joined the Panthers' sideline. By coincidence, he looked just like the player who had been thrown from the game, but he had a different number on his jersey. When this switch was pointed out to the referee, he told the Claremont players to focus on the game. The "new" player finished the game on the field and was a key reason the score remained close. Welsh chose not to make a big deal over Pierpont's underhand tactics, using the situation instead to remind his players of the right way to win and lose. He might have had a different attitude had Pierpont won the game, but it was not put to the test.

Kidder came to Claremont next, playing the first night game in Claremont's football history. Welsh's friends at Northern State Teachers College (formerly Northern Normal School) in Aberdeen had alerted him to the fact that the college was moving to a new venue and that the lights over Johnson Field were available should he want them for his field in Claremont. Welsh contacted Northern's athletic director, and they agreed on a price for the lights. The coach easily convinced the community to purchase the lights that he himself had played under while at Northern Normal. By the time the Kidder game came round, the fixtures were installed, and night football had arrived in little Claremont. In the ensuing contest, Kidder earned an early lead, but Gus Perkins took over and scored three touchdowns to secure the win. The Honkers' winning streak now stood at sixty. Following the Kidder game, the Honkers traveled to Roslyn, which had only recently started playing six-man football and had just joined the Lake Region Conference. As expected, Claremont beat them soundly.

With sixty-one wins under their belts, the Honkers could focus on the biggest game of the year—the upcoming rematch with archrival Hecla. Claremont's streak covered almost seven

years. They had set a national scoring record and had become
a regional phenomenon, receiving press coverage on a local,
regional, and national basis. They brought attention to a tiny
town in northeastern South Dakota and helped promote a game
that had reached its peak of popularity with over six thousand
teams competing across the country. Claremont *was* six-man
football in 1953, and with two games remaining, the Honkers
hoped to extend that status into 1954.

The Hecla Rockets, meanwhile, had blossomed into a force,
and the team had been undefeated since its last contest with
Claremont. No other team had played the Honkers more
times, and no team had suffered more defeats at their hands.
Including Claremont's first game in 1947, the Rockets had an
0–8 record against the Honkers, and none of the games had
been close. The 1953 game would be played at night, when even
more fans could flock to see the much-hyped game. The media
estimated the crowd watching the contest that night to be close
to two thousand, and the line for tickets formed a full twelve
hours before the game began.

As the players took the field, the Rockets wore a determined
look. Six years of defeat at the hands of Claremont's talented

In 1953,
this group
of young
men set the
national
record of
sixty-one
wins in a row.
*Welsh Family
Collection*

teams had made them angry. Both teams went through their warm-ups, but Hecla showed more enthusiasm and energy, and the Honkers realized that Hecla was not intimidated this time. The Claremont faithful noticed that same look, and they, too, realized that the Rockets had every intention of taking the crown from the champs. The crush of two thousand spectators and the palpable anticipation made it hard to breathe. The opening kick broke the mounting tension, and as the ball drifted towards Hecla's goal line, a diminutive halfback by the name of Delbert Schwarting caught the twirling ball and crowded in behind his blockers. The Honkers closed in on him, but Schwarting broke to the outside, evading his would-be tacklers. He picked up speed and galloped down the sideline, stunning the Honkers by scoring a touchdown the first time Hecla touched the ball. Rarely had the Claremont faithful seen another team take the early momentum in a game. In fact, during the previous sixty-one games, Claremont had trailed on just a handful of occasions.

Hecla lined up for the next kickoff, and Owen and Gus Perkins dropped back to receive the football. The kick went high into the air, and Owen called out that he had it. But as it drifted towards the younger brother, he took his eye off the ball for a second, looking for his path downfield. Having lapsed in concentration for just a moment, Owen found the ball slipping between his hands and bouncing high into the air. The swift Hecla defenders pounced on the fumble so quickly that Owen had no time to react, and Hecla ended up with the ball on the Honkers' two-yard line. On the next play, Hecla scored their second touchdown of the game. Two plays, two touchdowns. The fans of the Honkers had never seen anything like it, and neither had the players. The huge shift in momentum and the deep deficit against this strong, fired up Hecla team put Welsh's boys in uncharted territory. Stunned, the Honkers simply did not recover in time to wrest the momentum back. Not accustomed to playing catch up, and rocked from their foundation, the Claremont players could not right themselves again. Hecla's Schwarting scored three touchdowns that night, while stiff defense held the high-scoring Honkers to a shutout. The final count was 26 to 0.

The streak had ended, and the fans and players from Hecla went crazy in celebration. At last, they had achieved their goal and proven they could defeat the best in the country. The scene was indescribable, and somehow it was appropriate that the team the Honkers had defeated to start their sixty-one game streak was the team to beat the Honkers in the end. The loss hurt, but the Honkers were made of stern stuff. They were a classy group of boys whose coach had taught them to respect their opponents and the game, no matter what. Despite their disappointment, they embraced their defeat as an opportunity to show just how gracious they could be in a loss.

The final whistle blew, and sportswriter Al Neuharth, in the crowd that night, noted that each Honker quickly stepped to the nearest Rocket, shaking his hand and congratulating him on a game well-played. Both teams were aware of their impact on the history of the sport and shared in the moment. Moments earlier the teams had, according to Neuharth, been fighting like demons, but now they transformed into brothers. Every Claremont player agreed that they had lost to the better team. Bill

After the game, the scoreboard told the story. *Marc Rasmussen Collection*

Welsh made a point to seek out each Hecla player and coach and offer his sincere congratulations. The Claremont parents spontaneously decided to host a party for the victors after the game. It was a rare response, indeed, but it boiled down to what six-man football was all about—hard-working rural folks enjoying a common life experience, watching the children they loved compete.

Humbled, but by no means a bad team, Claremont started a new winning streak at Frederick the following week. This new string of successes lasted for two additional years, until the team finally fell victim to diminished enrollments at the school and could no longer field competitive football teams. In a nine-year span, from 1947 to 1955, Claremont won all but one game of six-man football, leaving them with the best winning percentage over that span of time of any team in the country. During those nine years, the Claremont Honkers' games were something the state press loved to cover. They enjoyed being a part of the "once-in-a-lifetime" streak. So few teams in the state's history could make a claim to national prominence, and it seemed that any South Dakota journalist who covered sports made at least one trip to watch the mighty Honkers play during its winning streak.

Bill Welsh, coach, teacher, promoter, and by this time Claremont school superintendent, had shown the world how the smallest of towns could succeed. The Armistice Day games, in particular, personified his promotional skills. By using the opportunity to create feature games every eleventh of November, the Claremont Honkers created a major sporting event in the region. Their state and region-wide challenge to play the best teams captured the imagination of the press and drew fans from as far away as Fargo, North Dakota, or Sioux Falls, South Dakota. With every win, Claremont football teams obtained respect across the state and region and gained incentive to perform at ever higher levels. However, Claremont's unbeaten run and eventual defeat by Hecla crowned the sport in South Dakota and, in many ways, signaled its apex as a national phenomenon. Eight- and nine-man football games were on the horizon, and Claremont's defeat was the beginning of a gradual demise of the sport in the Northern Great Plains.

# AFTER THE STREAK

**8** Not content with phenomenal success as a football coach, Bill Welsh applied his talents elsewhere both during and after the streak. Just as he had made the Armistice Day football games into a successful annual event, he also staged a holiday basketball tournament to which he invited some of the best teams in the area. Through an arrangement with KSDN Radio in Aberdeen, he could promise potential participants radio coverage of the games. Claremont paid a guarantee not just for the other teams but for the radio station, as well. KSDN broadcaster Dick Doyle was a welcome guest in Claremont. Rarely did a radio station leave its immediate market to do a remote broadcast from a small town, and this arrangement was one of the reasons the tournament attracted top-caliber teams. In so many ways, the success of the tournament was a tribute to the status Claremont had achieved in the region through Welsh's sporting success. The Honkers found that as long as they won games, people were interested in their story.

Although the 1953 football season ended sourly, Welsh immediately turned his attention to the basketball team to prepare them for the holiday tournament not far away. At the start of the season, Welsh had predicted that the team would be just average due to the graduation of some key players. This prediction contained a little psychology; he hoped it would push his young players to show their coach that they were much more than just average. The tactic worked, and the players put together an unexpected winning streak of their own that stretched to twenty-eight games and earned them a berth in the South Dakota State B basketball tournament. Coming in, they were the only undefeated basketball team in the state.

The 1954 State B tournament included the eight regional champions—Hayti, Selby, Delmont, Murdo, Lennox, Highmore, Provo, and Claremont—some of which perennially attended the event. The stars of the teams participating were well known throughout the state, and some would move on to successful college careers. In addition to Marv Rasmussen and Gus Perkins of Claremont, Maurie Hauglund, George Hurd, Dick Mudge, Garney Henley, Pepper Martin, Mike Poppens, Harvey Shaefer, Kay Besanson, Dan Goodman, and Tom Veren represented their teams admirably and were stars in their own right. The tournament took place in the Aberdeen civic arena in front of an overflow crowd. Nearly every man, woman, and child left Claremont and traveled en masse to Aberdeen to cheer for their Honkers, who opened against a strong team from Selby. Welsh's teams featured an aggressive man-to-man defense and a full court press designed to force opponents into giving up turnovers and taking bad shots. Selby countered this tactic with an exceptional guard who was able to break the press and get behind the defense with some long passes to players streaking down court. Claremont lost by just a few points, but the story might have been different had Welsh not suffered a medical issue.

According to his family, Welsh's car accident in 1952 had done more damage than he let on, and he lived in nearly constant pain. When he faced significant stress, blood would rush to his head, but for some reason, it did not clear as quickly as it rose. At the state tournament, the stress he felt caused this reaction, and he suffered such severe pain that he was unable to function normally. The players immediately noticed his difficulties, and his actions confused them during the game, when they could ill-afford to be distracted. Welsh's problems undoubtedly influenced the outcome of that first game against Selby. The pain was so intense that Welsh asked Edna to take him to the hospital after the game. She checked him into Saint Luke's Hospital, the same place she had received her nurse's training back in the 1920s.

With Welsh in hospital, the Columbia Comets' coach, Brad Hurin, and Bert Bernard, coach of the Britton Braves, offered to coach the Honkers in their second tournament game, this time against Lennox. Claremont won the game in overtime by a score of 50 to 44. Many who watched ranked it as the most exciting game of the tournament. The lead changed hands eight times, and neither team led by more than five points until near the end. In the consolation final against Murdo, both teams battled like champions for the entire game. Murdo came back from a fourteen-point deficit midway through the third quarter and then took the lead near the end of the final quarter. The two teams went through four lead changes until fouls mounted, and the game shifted to the free-throw line. Murdo had a one-point lead with two minutes remaining. Sensing victory, the Murdo coach instructed his players to stall for the end. With no shot clock, the tactic could prove effective, and the rest of the points scored came from foul shots. Murdo, performing the stall perfectly, ended up on the strong side of a 61–57 score, and the Honkers took home a sixth-place trophy.

During 1953 and 1954, Welsh saw the end of his six-man football winning streak, a near-perfect basketball season, another strong performance by the track squad, and *SoDak Sports* named him the High School Coach of the Year. He had accomplished more in his seven-and-a-half years at Claremont than many coaches accomplish in their entire careers. It might be difficult to understand why he now felt the need to move on, but Bill Welsh did just that. During his final two years at Claremont, he had suffered from debilitating head pain. The headaches were getting worse, and stress seemed to trigger these with greater frequency. The pressures of coaching were becoming detrimental to his health. In addition, building a legendary program leaves no room for anything else. The community expected greatness, and Welsh found himself missing the fun in coaching. He wanted to get back to the simple joy of coaching and working with young men. The State B tournament finally

## SoDak Sports Stars

by G.HALL

### Bill WELSH

GUIDING HAND FOR THE
NATIONALLY FAMOUS
**CLAREMONT HONKERS..**

**SODAK SPORTS**
HIGH SCHOOL
**COACH OF THE YEAR!**
1953-54

WELSH HAS COMPILED HIS AMAZING RECORDS IN A HIGH SCHOOL WHICH AVERAGES **ONLY 35 STUDENTS!**

COACH SAYS HE STILL DOESN'T NEED US!

THIS YEAR HE HAD **ONLY 18 BOYS IN HIGH SCHOOL!**

WELSH'S CLAREMONT HONKERS RAN THEIR SIX-MAN FOOTBALL VICTORY STREAK TO **61** LAST FALL....
...**AN ALL-TIME NATIONAL RECORD!!** THE STRING WAS FINALLY BROKEN BY UECLA, BUT WELSH'S SEVEN-YEAR FOOTBALL RECORD AT CLAREMONT NOW READS.. **62 WINS, 1 DEFEAT!**

AFTER THE FOOTBALL STRING RAN OUT, WELSH STARTED HIS BASKETBALL HONKERS ON A VICTORY PARADE... HIS CAGERS WON **28 IN A ROW** THIS YEAR BEFORE LOSING FIRST GAME IN STATE "B" TOURNEY.

WELSH IS A PRIME EXAMPLE OF A COACH WHO WINS BALL GAMES AND BUILDS CHARACTER, AT THE SAME TIME...
G.Hall

* * *          * * *

## Welsh Does Most With Least

A decade ago in Forrest City, Ia. a 5-year-old boy, the only son of Mr. and Mrs. Bill Welsh, was struck by a car and killed. Since then Coach Bill Welsh has devoted his every effort to developing the kind of athletes and gentlemen he had hoped his son might be.

His record of success is written indelibly at Claremont, where for seven years he has done "the most with the least." He brought national acclaim to a high school with an average of less than 20 boy students".

Welsh's closest "Coach of the Year" competition came from Floyd Mitchell of Parkston; Jim Marking of Hayti; Howard Taplett of Tyndall; Glenn Burgess of Deadwood, and Lars Overskei of Yankton.

*SoDak Sports* magazine named Bill Welsh its High School Coach of the Year for 1953–1954. *Welsh Family Collection* convinced Welsh that he had to find a more sedate life, one in which he could have more time for his family and approach coaching as a vocation, not as a lifestyle. As in so many situations before, Welsh had a hard choice between leaving these young men behind and his personal well-being. Welsh had grown to love the little town of Claremont and the support of its people, but he had also begun to wonder if their support might be contingent on his ability to continue winning. He recalled the old adage about the virtues of leaving at the top of your game. In the spring of 1954, Welsh announced his decision to leave Claremont.

Welsh's successor, Arlie Steen, inherited a seasoned and skillful bunch of athletes. Like Welsh, Steen was a product of Northern State Teachers College and had been an athlete of note there, starring as a tackle on the Wolves' football teams during the early 1950s. Also like his predecessor, he had had his career interrupted by a serious car accident in October 1951, in which he suffered a skull fracture. Steen only coached in Claremont for one year, but he enjoyed success nonetheless. He recognized the value of Welsh's programs and made few changes, leading the Honkers to another undefeated year in football, a conference championship in basketball, and a great showing in track.

Having decided to leave, Welsh accepted the head basketball and assistant football coaching jobs at Fergus County High School in Lewistown, Montana. The new positions offered him a chance to move into a program in an area of the country he thought absolutely beautiful; plus, he did not have to live up to the expectations created by his success in Claremont. He needed the change to give his head injury some time to heal, and a stepped-down role would keep his blood pressure at a more manageable level. His résumé helped him negotiate a good salary, and a fresh start as an assistant coach meant that he could use his accumulated knowledge of football in an advisory role without having to carry all the stress of a head coach.

Edna and his doctors approved. Lewistown was also a much larger community than Claremont, which meant an end to six-man and a return to coaching eleven-man football.

Welsh and his family enjoyed the mountains, and he welcomed the opportunity to work in an established program rather than having to create one from scratch. He brought a great degree of competence to the school, and the boys found themselves drawn to his calm, confident manner. With the head coach of the football team, he revamped the team's approach to the game. He helped with the fundamental development of the players and suggested new exercises and training techniques to prepare them physically for the game, and he continued to bring talented underclassmen into the varsity program at every opportunity. As he had done in his previous programs, he energized the fan base and generated excitement about the team.

Lewistown faced a tough schedule in 1954, but it still won a majority of its games. As the year went on, the young squad gained experience, and they all looked forward to their 29 October match-up at home against the much larger Gallatin High School of Bozeman. Bozeman's football team had strung together a good year and, with the help of their star player and co-captain Robert ("Rip") Van Winkle, looked like the team destined to win the conference. The night of the game came, and fans from Bozeman arrived early to get good seats, and they were soon joined by the hometown supporters.

Early in the game, Bozeman established its dominance and built a lead. Just before halftime, while Lewistown marched down the field, Van Winkle collided head-on with a Lewistown blocker and was rushed to the local hospital, where he was reported to be unconscious with spinal and head trauma. Three days later, without regaining consciousness, Robert Van Winkle became the first recorded casualty of a high-school football player during competition in the history of Montana. In the following week, Lewistown's head coach resigned for personal reasons, and the principal asked Welsh to coach the final game of the season. Welsh had mixed feelings about taking the team to Miles City for the game, as Van Winkle's death had affected the players and, for him personally, had opened up some old wounds surrounding the death of his son. Nevertheless, Welsh summoned up his deep reserves of strength and willpower to get him through what would be the last game in his career as a head football coach.

Slowly putting the season and the tragedy behind him, Welsh moved on to basketball. He had a good year with the team, but he also discovered the downside of being a basketball coach in Montana's class AA ranks. Given the sparse population in the huge state and the distance between schools of Lewistown's size, basketball teams traveled many miles and hours to play. Welsh found that he had even less time with his family than before, which was not what he had hoped for in this new position. By the end of the season, he decided not to finish his career at Lewistown and began to look around for other job opportunities.

What caught his eye was a chance to become an innkeeper again. He found a motel for sale overlooking the Middle Fork River, just seven miles from Glacier National Park, between the communities of Coram and Martin City, Montana. He and Edna decided to buy it, and at the end of the school year, Welsh resigned from his position at Lewistown. They named their new property Welsh's Pink Motel due to its unique color scheme. As they had done in Claremont, the family had to undertake some fix-up work before the business could accept guests, but the Welshes had finally found the perfect location. Bill and Edna operated the motel during the summer months when tourist travel was heavy; then, in the fall, the family moved to White-fish, eighteen miles north, where Bill taught industrial arts at the high school, and Edna worked as a nurse at the hospital.

The tranquility of the Welshes' life would be shattered one more time, however, during their early years at Welsh's Pink Motel. Years later, Patty Welsh Johnson recalled the summer afternoon when Billie Welsh got hit by a car. "She and I had been sitting inside our home, looking at a catalog, . . . picking out clothes and toys that we loved and [pretending] that we were buying them," she remembered. Her dad had finished his work and was sitting on a chair in the front yard reading the paper. "I recall that Mom was cooking supper," Patty wrote, when her father "asked Billie and me to turn on the neon lights as the afternoon sun began to fade. . . . I agreed to switch on the lights in the six units onsite while Billie would run directly across the road to turn on the neon sign that pointed to our motel. There was a slight curve in the road by the motel, which would make oncoming traffic from that one direction a bit difficult to see." Patty Welsh turned on the lights on three cabins, and then "heard a terrible screeching sound." Screaming, she ran to the front yard, "pulling my hair and crying. Dad was pulling Billie from under the car that had hit her." Edna and Bill nursed their stricken child as best they could while waiting for an ambulance.

The Welsh family faced the real prospect of losing another of its children. Bill and Edna were numb. Billie was in a coma, and the doctors were not sure she would survive. She sustained numerous broken bones and substantial lacerations. Internal injuries continued to be a real possibility, and the doctors could only treat the most acute injuries while they waited for Billie's response. As they had done anytime they faced adversity, the family came together, showed their strength, and pulled through the crisis. "I knew Billie's condition was grave, and I recall plugging my ears every time I heard Dad come home from the hospital, for fear of what he would have to say," Patty Welsh recalled. "Mom and Dad stayed with Billie around the clock. Jane took a quarter off from college. She came home to help, and . . . someone was with Billie 100 percent of the time." Bill Welsh maintained a calm exterior for the sake of the family, but in a candid moment with his oldest daughter Jane, he broke down, saying: "It can't happen again; it can't happen again."

Billie's injuries were profound, and her rehabilitation would take well over a year. Welsh became her physical therapist as she attempted to regain full motion of her limbs. Fortunately, Billie eventually recovered completely and suffered no lingering effects of the accident.

As Billie's health returned, Welsh enjoyed his final years of teaching and coaching at Whitefish. He became the head track coach at Whitefish High School and the assistant coach of both football and basketball. He enjoyed the boys he coached, the faculty, and the community, and he was happy with his roles within the athletic program. Whitefish was to be the last assignment in his career, and he coached and taught there until 1970. Coach Welsh finally announced his retirement at the age of sixty-seven.

Welsh dedicated his remaining years to his wife and family and put all he could into being the best grandfather he could be. When Bill passed away in 1980, his final wish was to be buried beside his son Jean in the small cemetery on the outskirts of Forest City, Iowa. Within a few months, Edna joined him in death, and together they are interred beside their son. Brother had been alone in a strange place for a long time, and this final act fulfilled the vow Bill had made so many years earlier.

In the 1940s, Bill Welsh was the right man in the right place at the right time. A man of exceptional character and compassion, he possessed a love of sport exceeded only by his love of family and of those young men fortunate enough to benefit from his mentorship and direction. Once injured in college, Welsh had drifted towards coaching as a practical career choice. By becoming a coach and educator, he melded his passion for athletics with a profession that could support his family. His son's untimely death eventually pushed Welsh towards the little South Dakota town of Claremont. Attempting to heal the emotional wounds incurred by Jean's death, Welsh found himself in the right place at the right time for both the school and himself. Determined to use his gift for coaching, and as a means of coping with his loss, Welsh built the most successful six-man football program in the country from the ground up.

Part of his success came from his choosing to embrace innovation when it could benefit his school and community. He found opportunities to succeed when others found excuses to fail, and he used his tenacious nature towards that end. Welsh's exposure to big-time athletics at the University of Illinois provided him with an understanding of the possibilities offered by football. By promoting a game, by finding the drama in a contest, and by selling that drama, he could excite not just his players but an entire community, particularly one as small as Claremont. Welsh's basic coaching philosophy, his belief in including underclassmen, and his firm, but fair mentoring, all contributed to the rise of the Claremont Honkers in six-man football. In the 1930s, Claremont had fielded an eleven-man football team but had cut the program by the end of the decade because the school could not consistently field a team. When

Stephen Epler created six-man football, small schools such as Claremont (and many others in South Dakota) could once again send their young men out onto the gridiron. Claremont's incredible run helped fuel the interest in a sport that perfectly suited small high schools in the region.

Not only did Welsh create a successful sporting legacy at Claremont, he also overcame difficult times in his personal life. He carried his family through harrowing episodes, maintaining a veneer that hid his deep emotional and physical wounds. When the final score was tallied at the end of his life, Bill Welsh had achieved so much more than his impressive accomplishments as a coach. Nevertheless, his impact on the game of football in the state of South Dakota has left its own indelible mark. In South Dakota, from the beginning to the end of Claremont's winning streak, the number of teams participating in the sport increased from a few dozen to over one hundred fifty. During those seven unbeaten years, Claremont played sixty-one "championship" games against teams intent on emulating the Honkers. Every team facing the champs during their record run wanted their shot at ending the streak, and every team but one felt the sting of defeat. The quest to beat the Honkers and the increased number of participants in the sport of six-man football led to a higher quality of play in each subsequent season. Inevitably, the quality of the teams increased to a point where there was real parity among teams in the region. By 1953, no team could score nearly one hundred points against a weaker opponent, and the margins of victory declined each year, making games even more exciting.

Claremont's winning streak ended at a time of change in rural South Dakota. Many ultra-small communities, battered by the economic environment and out-migration of population, could no longer support the cost of a high school, and the number of secondary schools began a steady decline as more and more communities chose to join together to create larger school districts with one school. Communities with a critical mass of students that could provide adequate funding to keep the doors open found that the six-man game had run its course. With each subsequent closure of a small school, the number of potential opponents declined. As a consequence of consolidation, schools had more boys able to play football, but in many cases, still not quite enough to field competitive eleven-man teams. As a result, eight-man and then nine-man versions took the place of six-man football in South Dakota. Today, the six-man variant has been redefined, and Texas is the undisputed king of the sport. Small towns in the Lone Star State have taken six-man to new heights, creating new legends and new records. Time has improved the game, and it remains one of the most interesting derivatives of the sport.

For much of the country, six-man had been the sport of choice for small communities for thirty years from the 1930s and even now, almost sixty years later, those fortunate enough to have been fans or participants remember it fondly. In many ways, Bill Welsh was the face of the sport of six-man football in those early years. During his tenure as the Honkers' coach, ninety-one different athletes and cheerleaders contributed to the national record. Welsh helped a tiny town in the middle of nowhere become relevant and left a winning spirit that the sons and grandsons of the Honkers players continue to bear proudly. Welsh's lifetime record in football was 137 wins, 15 losses, and 3 ties, and in basketball his record was 375 wins to 58 losses. As a coach of six-man football, Welsh enjoyed a record second-to-none. Welsh's Claremont football teams won 62 games and suffered just the single loss. His lifetime winning percentage as a six-man coach was an amazing 98.4 percent, and for six-man coaches with more than sixty wins, Welsh had no equal in that category.

For his abilities, Welsh received awards both during his lifetime and after. In 1950, he received an honorary membership in the Sports Trail Century Club, organized by a *Chicago Times* writer for coaches who had at least one hundred wins to their name. He was selected as *SoDak Sports* Honorary Coach of the Six-Man Football All-Star Team in 1953; as *SoDak Sports* High School Coach of the Year in 1953–1954; and as a presenter at the All-American Coaching Clinic in Bemidji, Minnesota, in June 1955. Since his death, he has been elected to the South Dakota Football Coaches Association Hall of Fame (2001), the South Dakota High School Athletic Coaches Association Hall of Fame (2002), the National High School Coaches Association Hall of Fame (2005), and the South Dakota Sports Hall of Fame (2008). Moreover, he demonstrated that one man could energize a program and create excellence from raw material. Most importantly, however, Welsh was a special man with a unique gift for teaching and inspiring teenage boys to succeed beyond all expectations.

## CLAREMONT HONKERS' SIX-MAN FOOTBALL TEAM
## COMPLETE RECORD, 1947–1953

**1947**
vs. Hecla 43–6
vs. Leola 31–22
vs. Webster (11 v 11) 44–7
vs. Barnard 45–0
vs. Leola 32–6
vs. Hecla 57–7
vs. Barnard 47–0
vs. Montrose 40–24

**1948**
vs. Hecla 58–6
vs. Barnard 69–0
vs. Wilmot 60–0
vs. Webster B (11 v 11) 38–0
vs. Hecla 63–6
vs. Selby 68–14
vs. Browns Valley 65–41
vs. Faith 77–30
vs. Langford 68–6
vs. Hankinson 40–0

**1949**
vs. Barnard 46–7
vs. Wilmot 71–13
vs. Kidder 62–32
vs. Bristol 58–11
vs. Pierpont 28–20
vs. Selby 39–0

vs. Browns Valley 60–19
vs. Langford 77–14
vs. Hecla 31–19

**1950**
vs. Barnard 46–0
vs. Langford 87–6
vs. Kidder 50–0
vs. Bristol 80–13
vs. Plankinton 28–8
vs. Pierpont 72–10
vs. Linton 72–0
vs. Java 78–19
vs. Hecla 72–19

**1951**
vs. Waubay 70–0
vs. Plankinton 39–24
vs. Frederick 94–49
vs. Columbia 53–20
vs. Bristol 64–24
vs. Pierpont 56–26
vs. Langford 57–7
vs. Hecla 50–14

**1952**
vs. Waubay 37–6
vs. Langford 47–7
vs. Veblen 13–6

vs. Columbia (score unavailable)

vs. Bristol 38–31

vs. Pierpont 50–20

vs. Frederick (score unavailable)

vs. Isabel 31–14

vs. Hecla 49–12

**1953**

vs. Andover 53–21

vs. Waubay 60–19

vs. Veblen 13–12

vs. Columbia 38–13

vs. Bristol 46–13

vs. Pierpont 38–28

vs. Kidder (score unavailable)

vs. Roslyn (score unavailable)

vs. Hecla 0–26

vs. Frederick (score unavailable)

# BIBLIOGRAPHIC ESSAY

Due to the rural nature of the communities involved in this story, published materials are somewhat sparse. In addition to the interviews, scrapbooks, and other material mentioned in the preface, I utilized a large number of newspapers, which documented the Honkers' record and provided some insight into the variables that made Coach Welsh and his student athletes successful. Newspaperarchive.com was a conduit to much of the material via its searchable database of thousands of small-town newspapers throughout the United States. Through this resource, I accessed the pages of the *Daily Huronite* and the *Mitchell Daily Republic.* Newsbank.com gave me access to the *Aberdeen American News.* I also visited the Alexander Mitchell Library in Aberdeen, South Dakota, to view microfiche of missing issues of Brown County papers. Weekly newspapers from Groton, Claremont, and Hecla, available on microfilm from the State Archives Collection of the South Dakota State Historical Society in Pierre, supplied additional anecdotes and statistics. Many newspaper clippings are also available in the Mickey Vickers and Welsh family scrapbooks. The Claremont High School annuals from 1948, 1950, and 1952 added valuable flavor and statistics not found in the newspaper articles.

General history of the sport of football came from two internet sources, Wikipedia.com and the Walter Camp Foundation website. Information about Stephen Epler and his development of the game of six-man football can be found in a host of sources. Its widespread success resulted in coverage by newspapers all over the country. Epler was also famous for creating smaller versions of other popular games, for writing a controversial essay on the practice of awarding honorary degrees for the patrons of universities, and for founding Portland State University in Portland, Oregon. He received coverage in national periodicals including *American Boy*, *Life*, and *Time*. *Mechanix Illustrated* also featured him in a November 1938 article titled "Scientific Sports: Six-Man Football," by Ken Strong. The first mention of Epler appears in an article titled "Football" in the 14 October 1935 edition of *Time* magazine. An article titled "Sport: Six-Man," in the 11 October 1937 issue of the same publication, described the evolution of the game, its growing popularity, and how it fit the culture of the day. Epler's own booklet, *How to Play Six-Man Football*, published by General Mills, maker of Wheaties, in 1935, gave a brief history and set out the rules to play a low-contact version of the sport. Various newspapers across the country, such as the *Lebanon Daily News* (27 Sept. 1934) of Lebanon, Pennsylvania, the *Cumberland Evening Times* (25 Aug. 1939, 2 Jan. 1946) of Cumberland, Maryland, and *Big Spring Herald* (7 Oct. 1953) of Big Spring, Texas, chronicled the beginning and growth of the sport. In his article "Six-Man Football Is Still Very Big with Some Small American Towns," Merill Gilfillan reminisced about the sport and discussed those states still participating for *Sports Illustrated* (4 Nov. 1983).

The details of Welsh's college years were especially difficult to document, but with help from his daughters and newspaper articles detailing the Illinois sports program, Harold ("Red") Grange, Robert Zuppke, and Welsh's return to the Northern Normal College program, the story took form. The *Decatur Daily Review* and the *Aberdeen Daily American* proved especially valuable. Sports writer Grantland Rice's poem "Alumnus Football" appears on page 144 of his book *Only the Brave, and Other Poems* (New York: A. S. Barnes & Co., 1941). In an article titled "Grange, in Line For All-Star Honors, Is Just Learning the Game Asserts Zuppke," which appeared in the *Nevada State Journal* (28 Nov. 1923), Norman Brown writes of how Grange came to be a member of the Illinois team and of his relationship with Robert Zuppke. The *Lima News* (16 Dec. 1923) of Lima, Ohio, recounted the statistics and highlights of Grange's first All-American year.

Information about actor Julie Haydon came from newspaper articles that discussed her career and her Broadway performances including the *Salt Lake Tribune* (29 Sept. 1935), the *San Antonio Express* (3 Nov. 1935), and the *Portsmouth Times* (25 Sept. 1935) of Ohio. Welsh's time in Kimball, South Dakota, was documented from multiple sources, with assistance from head basketball coach Kamden Miller and the Kimball High School administration. In addition to my own research efforts, I received help from Billie Welsh Bartlett who had done substantial legwork in preparation for Welsh's induction into the National High School Coaches Hall of Fame. She had visited Kimball, where she had opportunity to talk with one of the players from her father's coaching era. Fred Houda and his wife, Lucille, provided a significant amount of background for those years. Woody Wentzy, writing for the *Kimball Graphic* and *the Kimball Star*, provided data on key games and the rivalry between Kimball and Chamberlain. The *Daily Huronite* and *Mitchell Daily Republic* also covered conference games.

Jim Block, principal/superintendent of Webster High School, provided access to important athletic records given to the South Dakota State High School Athletic Association. This data detailed the names of the athletes, the sports records for the year, scores, and a host of notes written by the coach. Bartlett had also investigated this era and referenced a number of sources. Among those providing data was Anne Fossum, librarian from the Webster Public Library. School annuals and newspaper articles from the *Daily Huronite* filled in the gaps.

For Welsh's two years at Forest City, Iowa, the local newspaper contained some, but not a lot of, information on the sports teams. Welsh's daughters loaned me articles that they had found in northern Iowa newspapers, including the *Mason City Gazette*, the *Council Bluffs Nonpareil*, the *Muscatine Journal and News-Tribune*, and the *Waterloo Daily Courier*. Also included in

Bartlett's scrapbook was an important article from the *Winnebago-Hancock Summit*, the local Forest City newspaper, detailing the events surrounding the death of Jean Welsh.

The most productive resources for the Claremont High School era were found in issues of *SoDak Sports* from its inception in 1952 until it went out of business in 1954. Published by Al Neuharth, later of Gannett Publishing, this newspaper was generations ahead of its time in the quality and detail of coverage, providing objective data and statistics along with Neuharth's editorial comments related to the national record-setting run. The *Aberdeen American News*, starting with its earliest predecessor the *Aberdeen Daily American*, provided solid coverage of sports in the region and was a key source of statistical and background data. For the flavor of the game, photographs, and other relevant data, the scrapbooks and memories of Ruby Vickers, Ramona Hurin, Delores Henihan, Marvin Rasmussen, and Harold ("Red") Sanderson were invaluable, as was the coffee crowd at Swede's Bar in Langford, South Dakota. Records provided by Monte Nipp, superintendent and principal of the Langford Public Schools, included a pamphlet from the Claremont Booster Club that detailed all the Claremont victories up to 1951. An *Aberdeen American News* article entitled "Honkers Still Rule Six-Man Football," on 21 November 1952, discussed the run up to the national record, talked about the Armistice Day games, and stressed the point that Claremont did not play "set up" games but challenged the best teams in the region.

The *Aberdeen American News* was also the source for information on the Honkers after Welsh's tenure, starting with an article titled "Welsh Takes Coaching Job in Montana" (15 July 1954). Coverage of Welsh's final years in coaching is hard to find outside of a few articles in the Lewistown, Bozeman, Billings, and Whitefish newspapers. The serious injury of Robert Van Winkle of Bozeman was described in an article in the *Billings Gazette* on 30 October 1954, and coverage of his death can be found in the *Daily Interlake* of Kalispell, on 2 November 1954.

# INDEX

Note: page numbers in italics refer to figures.

97, *141*; season of 1949, 102–5, *103*, *141*; season of 1950, 105–10, *106–9*, *141*; season of 1951, 110–14, *112*, *141*; season of 1952, 116–20, *117*, 117–18, *141–42*; season of 1953, 120–26, *123*, *141*; second string, 10; sportsmanship of, 125–26; success of, 138; team preparation and warm-up, 14–15; training by, 78; uniforms of, 6, 7; Welsh's building of program, 74; winning percentage, 126; winning streak, 7, 21, 92, 112, 113–14, 119–20, 122–127. *See also* Fans of Claremont Honkers

Claremont Honkers track team, 95, 101, *101*, 105, 115, 130

Clark High School, 52

Columbia Comets, 117, 121

Cornbelt Conference, 93

*Cumberland Times*, 87

Custer Battlefield Highway Conference, 42, 44

Cutler, Kay: and football season of 1947, 92, 94; and football season of 1948, 96; at reunion of 2003, xiii; on Welsh's coaching methods, 78

Cutler, Lyle: as baseball player, 100; as basketball player, 95, 100; and football season of 1947, 93–94; and football season of 1948, 96–97, 100; at reunion of 2003, xiii; role on team, 15; in student government, 100

Cutler, Val: and football season of 1947, 92, 94; and football season

of 1948, 100; and football season of 1949, 102, 105

Daly, Ramona, 16

Doland High School, 52

Doyle, Dick, 128

Earnest, Arch, 8

Edwards, Jane Welsh. *See* Welsh, Jane Katherine (daughter)

Epler, Stephen: *How to Play Six-Man Football*, 73, 86, *87*, 144; invention of six-man football, 82–86, 137–38, 143–144; and six-man football All-American team, 87

Erdahl, Elton, 63

Faith Longhorns, 9, 96, 99

Fans of Claremont Honkers: at Armistice Day Game (1948), 4, 11–12, 17–18; at Armistice Day Game (1953), 123; and attendance of out-of-town spectators, 9, 11, 75, 111–12, 126; and football season of 1949, 104; sportsmanship of, 20. *See also* Automobiles

Feller, Bob, *68*

Fergus County (Mont.) High School, Welsh's coaching career at, 132–34

Feser, Paul, 100, 102, 106, 110

Football, eight and nine-man: 127, 139

Football, eleven-man: dangers of, 35, 133; small-town schools' inability to participate in, 81–82

and Claremont football field, 74; and renovation of Welsh's Game Lodge, 69

Welsh, Willis ("Bill"): appearance, 28; awards received by, 130, *131*, 139–40; at banquet honoring winning streak, 114; birth and childhood, 27–28; car crash injuries (1952), 115, 129–30, *131*; cares for daughter Billie, 135–36; character and personality of, 9, 28, 61, 70, 137; and cheerleaders at Claremont, 18, 74; coaching style, 38–39, 41, 46–47, 75–78, 95, 114; college going-away celebration, 34; community involvement encouraged by, 2–3, 45–46, 47–48; death and burial, 136; death of son and its impact on, 14, 60–64, 137; decision to return to coaching, 70–72; early married life, 49–50; financial concerns, 49–50, 56; game-day preparations, 2–3, 5–6, 10; high-school athletic career, 28–31; impact on South Dakota football, 138; involvement of younger boys in program, 14, 133, 137; in Lake City, S.Dak., 71; lifetime record, 139; as motivator, 12–14, 46, 62, 75–78, 103–4; at Northern Normal College, *37*, 37–39, 41; photographs of, *43*, *51*, *55*, *58*, 97, *101*, *103*, *106*, *112*, *117*, *123*; plays designed by, 16–17; professionalism of, 41; promoting of events, 3, 7–8, 38–39, 47, 98, 107, 126, 128, 133, 137; relationship with Marvin Rasmussen, xi–xii; relationship with son, 52–53; and Red Grange, 32, 36, 72; retirement, 136; speaking engagements, 114; sports injuries, 36–37, 39, 137; sportsmanship of, 20, 121–22, 125–26; success, reasons for, 137; tragedies faced by, 138; University of Illinois recruitment and football career, 31–38; at Whitefish (Mont.) High School, 134–36; Zuppke's influence on, 38–39, 45–46, 47, 75, 137. *See also* Claremont Honkers football team; Fergus County (Mont.) High School; Forest City High School; Kimball High School; Webster High School

Welsh's Game Lodge: decision to buy, 63–64; described, 63; Edna's reaction to, 67; location, benefits of, 67–68; renovation of, 68–69; success of, 70

Welsh's Pink Motel, 134–36

Wentzy, Woody, 45, 145

Wheaties cereal, support for six-man football, 85, *87*, 144

Whitefish, Mont., 134, 136, 146

Whitefish (Mont.) High School, Welsh's teaching career at, 134–36

Wilmot High School, 97, 103

Zuppke, Robert ("The Little Dutchman"): influence on Welsh, 38–39, 45–47, 75, 137; at University of Illinois, 31–36, 144